GREENER FIELDS

BY THE AUTHOR

Ten Grandmothers

Winter-Telling Stories

Maria, the Potter of San Ildefonso

Indians on Horseback

The Valley Below

These Are the People

Indians of the Four Corners

Hell on Horses and Women

Greener Fields

ALICE *Lee* MARRIOTT

GREENER FIELDS

FIELDS

EXPERIENCES AMONG THE

AMERICAN INDIANS

THOMAS Y. CROWELL COMPANY
NEW YORK

970.1

For
Anthropology 102
2:00–4:30 P.M.

Chapters 8, 10, and 11 originally appeared, in somewhat different form, in *The New Yorker*.

CONTENTS

GREENER FIELDS

CHAPTER 1

THROUGH THE BACK DOOR

Most of the anthropologists I have known got into the business by way of the back door. Almost never, in my generation, did they start out to be anthropologists. Physical anthropologists began as geneticists or med students; archaeologists started out as anything from engineers to portrait painters; ethnologists began with a range that covered a field as wide as that which stretches between musicology and sociology. Nowadays, I hear, some youngsters enter school with archaeological bees firmly attached to their bonnets, but in this book I'm talking about twenty years ago.

I began as a librarian. According to my family I was a bright young thing, if rather homely, and my grandmother developed and passed on to my parents the idea that it would be nice for me to work in a library. Her theory was that a library would provide satisfactory employment because I liked to read and a librarian was surrounded with books. Also, she had observed that in libraries you could meet lots

1

of nice interesting people. I still like to read, and in the last twenty years I have met quantities of people who were both interesting and nice, but in a library catalog room I have never read any book for pleasure, and have seldom met anybody at all.

For that was where I fetched up. I made failing grades in cataloging all through my library-training course, and to this day I am fundamentally impatient of detail. But I graduated from college at a time when catalogers were needed and reference librarians weren't, and so I became a cataloger.

The town where I went to work was one hundred and sixty long miles from my home. I was barely twenty years old, and I was holding down a job that is usually entrusted to women of forty and upwards. I knew nobody, and was pathologically shy. All I had was a brain, and it was stretched to the breaking-point by unfamiliar and uncongenial tasks.

The country around the town was full of low, rolling hills separated from one another by streams that meandered mildly except in spring and fall, when they rose and invaded large portions of the town. This was eastern Oklahoma; the city had once been the capital of the Creek Indian Nation, and was in my time agency headquarters for what are generally known as the Five Civilized Tribes: the Cherokee, Choctaw, Chickasaw, Seminole, and Creek.

The head librarian had a passionate interest in history and genealogy, which expressed itself in the form of a collection of books on local history, which in that town meant Indian history. It fell to me to catalog the books, and, subsequently, to index their contents. The indices completed, I discovered in myself an interest in the subjects it covered. With the head librarian's blessing and consent—at a time when she was hurrying to a D.A.R. meeting—I took over the ordering as well as the organization of the Indian collection.

2

About that time the usual spring flood took place, to be succeeded by the usual spring crop of mosquitoes. Among them was that hardy southerner—*anopheles.* By the time my mother got me home that fall I was a skeleton, alternately blazing and shaking with the seizures of the most unpleasant type of diurnal malaria, which was well-rooted in my blood stream.

When the next spring rolled around I was physically better, but mentally not in good shape. This was in 1932 and employment, even for librarians with degrees, training, and experience, was pitifully scarce. Nevertheless, I needed a job. My few savings were gone, my parents had three children younger than I to finish high school and enter college, and my duty was clear. It was time I went to work.

So I wandered into the State Library Commission, where a friend of mine was head cataloger. My intention was simple: a coke and a bit of gossip might lead to the naming of a town which needed a librarian. My friend was hospitable, but busy.

"Sit down," she urged, pushing a stack of new books at me. "Just go over these and classify them, so I can get through. Then we'll go for a coke. They're easy—run through them and give them the general classifications."

I have never before tried to describe exactly what happened when I opened the first book, and I may not succeed now. The title page was completely blank at first. Then, as I watched it, hieroglyphics began to form. They were, to me, mysterious and unreadable. I turned to my friend.

"What language are these written in?" I asked her. "Is there a translated title page somewhere?"

"Why," she said without looking up, "they're all in English, of course. This is the new lot of children's books."

I got out of there quickly and onto a streetcar and down

to the doctor's office. I wasn't sure what had happened to me, but I was sure that I needed medical care, and in a hurry. Bursting into the office, I incoherently sobbed out the story of the past hour. The doctor listened as well as he could, and then made me repeat the tale. Then he produced a glass of water and a mild sedative, and suggested that I draw a deep breath.

When I had calmed down somewhat, the doctor provided further comfort in the form of common sense. What had happened to me was nothing unusual. Mild amnesias of this type frequently befall people. What I needed to do was to put my condition to good use, and forget the whole incident.

"Did you really like cataloging?" he inquired.

I raised my head from his desk with a jerk. The question was one I would never have dared ask myself. Did I really *like* cataloging? The answer was written in the air before me in letters of fire.

"No!" I gasped. "I've always hated it!"

"Are you very fond of any kind of library work?" was the next question.

"No," I sniffed, "not very." My head dropped to his desk again. I wept aloud. "But it's all I know how to do," I wailed. "And I've *got* to earn a living. I'm twenty-three!"

Knowing that doctor as well as I do now, I suspect that he grinned. But his voice, when I heard it, was entirely calm, and that was what I needed.

"I think," the doctor said judiciously, "that there still might be time for you to learn another trade. You come of a long-lived family, I have reason to know. Right now, what you need to do is to get your mind off your troubles. What do you like to do with your hands?"

"I like to cook," I sobbed.

"And with your mind? Is there anything besides libraries that you're particularly interested in?"

I raised my head, startled, and stared at the man. The surprise came from within me, and was directed at myself. "Yes," I said, suddenly quieted, "I'm interested in Indians."

If the choice impressed the doctor as odd, he didn't show how he felt. "Well," he said, "the University of Oklahoma has a department of anthropology now. Perhaps, if you're well enough, you can enroll next fall. Here's a diet list. Go home, and have as much fun as you can cooking the things on it, and eating them. If you gain ten pounds on your own cooking by September, you can go to school."

I am sure the doctor must have communicated with my parents, but no one said anything about amnesia to me. I went home and cooked and cooked and ate and ate, and worked my way up *almost* to a hundred pounds. (I am five and a half feet tall, and big-boned.) And by fall, although I was still more than a pound short of my goal, I was rewarded. I was allowed to go to the university, twenty miles away, and enroll for three hours of class work a week.

Enrollment was not so simple as it had been for me in my undergraduate days. Now I was to enroll as a "graduate-special," not working towards a degree, but still attending classes for credit. To do so, I must first obtain the permission of the head of the anthropology department.

With some difficulty, I located the office of the department of anthropology. (I have since learned that all anthropolgy offices are automatically located in whatever equivalent of a cellar or garret a given university possesses.) I knocked timidly on the office door, which stood ajar, and stepped across the threshold. A boy sat at a typewriter by the window.

"I'd like to see the professor," I hazarded.

"He isn't here," the boy answered, entirely uninterested in me.

"When will he be here?"

"I don't know for sure. Maybe some time tomorrow; maybe not till the next day."

"Where *is* he?" I demanded.

"Out in the field; hasn't come in from the summer dig yet."

I returned to the office of the graduate school and explained the situation. The office personnel was adamant. I *must* see the professor and obtain his permission to enroll before they could do anything further. If I hadn't seen the professor and obtained his permission within three days when class sessions were to begin, I would be charged a late enrollment fee. My parents were financing my return to college. The thought of their spending extra money panicked me. I got on the interurban and went home, dramatically and in my own mind giving up the whole idea.

The next day I again got on the interurban and went back to the university. I was *damned* if I'd give up so easily. If my mother and father were willing to bet on me, I certainly should be willing to bet on myself. As the old-fashioned, high, unstable, smelly trolley rocked along I began to get mad; first at myself for being a quitter, then at the professor for making me want to quit.

The professor was not in his office. The secretary, still busily typing by the window, had not heard from him. I walked out and took the next interurban home, too mad to eat dinner that night since it did not consist entirely of nails.

There was no professor in the office the next day, either.

A lot of things have happened to me since then. Since then I have learned about sacred numbers. I have learned from my Indian friends that in many tribes, in order to suc-

6

ceed in anything really important, you must make three tries and three failures before the fourth, finally successful, attempt.

The professor was in his office the fourth day. He was slumped comfortably back in a swivel chair, with his feet on his desk.

"Hello," he said amiably when I appeared in the doorway, "what do you want?"

The boy at the typewriter glanced up at me. "She's the one I was telling you about," he explained. "Wants permission for graduate enrollment."

The professor swiveled his head, but not his chair, and looked at me again. "Why?" he inquired. No interest, no feeling, no nothing. Just—"why?"

"Because I can't enroll without it," I snapped, getting madder than I had ever known I could.

"Why enroll?" the professor demanded flatly.

"I want to know something about Indians!" I stormed.

I entered the doorway for the first time in all those endless days, and slammed the enrollment card down on the desk before my inquisitor. Still with his feet above his head, he picked up the card and looked at it.

"You can't enroll in these courses," the professor then announced serenely. "They're for upper-division credit."

"I'd like to know why not!" I bristled. "I'm a graduate student. I ought to be able to take junior and senior courses."

The professor laid the card on the desk, and sighed delicately.

"For more years than I would admit even to my sainted mother," he proclaimed oracularly, "I have waited for a student to walk in here and say what you said just now—'I want to take a course in anthropology so I can learn something about Indians.' Now the time has come. If you want

7

to learn something about Indians in this department, you will have to begin at the beginning. You can start at the bottom, with Anthropology One—that's the freshman course—and go as far as your furious absorption in Indians will carry you. I will not approve these upper-division courses for your enrollment at present. I will only approve the beginning course. Go on over to the dean's office and tell them so. Tell them to call me, if they don't believe you."

I marched stiffly out of the office and across the campus to the administration building, burning with fury. Still I was perfectly sure the graduate-office personnel would back me up in my demand for upper-division courses. Instead, they backed the professor.

The following morning found me sitting rigidly in the front row of the Anthropology One class, with my near-sighted eyes riveted on the blackboard. The professor entered and greeted me beamingly.

"I see you changed your mind," he remarked cordially. I could feel myself scorching all over, right down to the seat of my chair.

The rest of this account may sound a little like a success story, and will therefore be unfashionably out of date. Anyhow I stayed in that classroom. At first because I loathed the professor; later because, like all his serious students, I came to reverence that extraordinary man. I worked my head off. I made straight A's. I shone. And, as my temper fit wore away and the real fascination of the field of anthropology took hold of me, I came to see the subject not only as one that was of extreme academic interest, but also as a way of life.

Behind the classroom work, behind the patching and piecing of broken pots in the laboratory, behind the regrettable occasion when three of us dissected, cleaned, boiled down, and reassembled a skeleton from a cadaver, there was a philosophy that could be summed up as: To know is to understand, to understand is to accept. And to accept is to perceive that racial and cultural differences are quite literally only skin deep.

"There, but for the Grace of God, go I," is a misquotation that has been worn thin, that has acquired an aura of unbearable smugness. "There, but for an accident of Nature, I go," would be nearer to the philosophy I learned, and learned to practice, as a student of anthropology. And even that rephrasing does not quite express the attitude we were taught to cultivate for ourselves. Not only all men, but all cultures, had been created equal; equal in interest, equal in complexity at one point or another, equally, as our world says, high.

They were not to be compared, only to be studied and described. And some of us tried mightily to shed our prejudices and to achieve the balance of outlook this belief implied. If at times, we ran the danger of regarding our own culture as inferior to others *because* it was our own, we could be jerked out of our attitude of humility—a healthy one for the young in any case—by being reminded that no culture was lower, as none was higher, than others.

By the second semester of that school year I was taking twelve hours a week of classroom work, and spending every spare hour I could find in the laboratory. Not only were my grades good, I had gained seven pounds, for now I ate whatever I could lay hands on whenever I was able to locate it.

One day I was called to the professor's office.

"What are you planning to do this summer?" he asked, his feet on the desk and a printed sheet in one hand.

"Why—I don't know," I answered. I was so engrossed with the present that I had forgotten the future was only six weeks away.

"You're a problem," the professor observed thoughtfully. "It's evident you've got the makings of an anthropologist. I'll approve your enrollment for a major next fall, when the time comes. But you are the only woman major this department's had so far. All the rest are male."

"I don't see—" I began, but he cut me off.

"The major field emphasis of this department, as at present organized, is archaeology," its head continued. "I take the major students out on summer digs. We live in tents, we cook for ourselves or hire a Negro boy if we can find one, and we work like fools."

"I don't mind—" I started again.

"No, but the boys do," the professor interrupted. "I've already had three of them in here asking if they've got to have a girl around this summer. They aren't pleased with the idea."

"I can do better repair work than any of them, and you said yourself that catalog system I worked out could be applied in the field," I protested.

"Keep your hair on," the head of the department said soothingly. "Sometimes I can see the boys' point of view," he added philosophically. "However, you like people, and you seem to get along with them."

"I hate people, and I'm scared to death of them," I argued vigorously.

"Then why do you think it's a good idea to spend a summer stuck in the woods with a mess of them you've been seeing all winter?"

"Well—I— Well, I—I'm used to them!"

"I'm sorry," the professor's voice was determined. "All this time the department has lacked something, and you're going to be it. Get over to the hat rack and tie yourself to the stake, you're going to be sacrificed. What we need around here is an ethnology major, and you're elected."

"Kinship!" I sneered.

"Kinship systems and terminology," the professor agreed.

"The Maya calendar," I moaned.

"The most perfect and complicated astronomical system the mind of man has yet achieved," he murmured dreamily.

"Weaving. Pottery. Stone working. Material culture generally," I enumerated.

"*What* the hell else is archaeology?" the professor demanded, finally losing *his* temper. "Now, you look here! We've got to keep you busy during the summer so you won't lose interest. Here's a fellowship announcement from a foundation, and an application form. Sit down and look over one and fill out the other, and we'll stick the application in the mail tonight. The department will even provide a stamp, to encourage you. Probably you won't get the award, but it's worth a few cents to find out."

I never doubted that I would get the fellowship. It never entered my mind to doubt. The alternative, as far as I could see, would be sudden death from disappointment, and so I did not face the alternative. Surely if the Lord had restored my sanity and will to live, He would not leave the job half-done. Nor did He. I got the award.

My parents had so far been amused and tolerant about everything. They favored any occupation to keep their child healthily, happily, occupied. But when I came home from the university one day and informed them that I was leaving for Oregon in a month, to meet a party of strangers recruited from other universities in other parts of the country, and live in a tent, their eyes glazed and they were struck temporarily speechless.

By the time they recovered their voices, I was in such a whirl of preparations and so overwhelmed with anticipation that they did not attempt to argue with me. Instead, my father bought me a canvas sleeping bag as a going-away present, and my mother, half sure that she would never see her oldest child alive again, helped me pack. I was on the train and on the way before I fully realized that, for the first time in my adult life, I was going outside my home state.

The last thing I did before departure was call the doctor and tell—not ask—tell him what I was about to do.

"Have a good time," the doctor said by way of farewell blessing.

I went, and I had it, and I have been having it ever since.

CHAPTER 2

THE DOWNTRODDEN, ETC.

M Y very first field work in ethnology was not done in Oklahoma. I went as one of a group of students chosen from universities all over the United States, to work under one of the country's leading ethnologists, in southern Oregon. The tribe which was at our mercy belonged to the general Plateau culture area. The Indians of this section are said to be hostile in their attitude towards whites, and secretive in their attitude towards their own culture. They keep themselves *to* themselves, to employ a time-honored phrase, and they do not welcome strangers, nor talk freely to those whom they consider intruders.

Luck was with me, for it was sheer luck that sent me Mary Many Feathers as my first informant and as the first Indian woman with whom I worked in close association. The local Indian Agency supplied a group of names of possible informants and interpreters, and I drew Mary, literally, out of a hat.

Two phrases will always remind me of Mary Many Feathers, by contrast. They are, "The downtrodden Indian squaw," and, "The filthy Indian." Even if I had been one to refer to a friend with the wildly inappropriate word "whore," which is the practical equivalent of "squaw," I could never —under any circumstances—have regarded Mary as downtrodden. As for filth, she was one of the most compulsively immaculate housekeepers I have ever known. She and her surroundings shone, and her clothes wore threadbare as the result of repeated scrubbings.

"I went to Carlisle and was raised by the Friends," she said to me early in our acquaintance. "Naturally, I keep things around me nice. 'They'd' be disappointed if I didn't."

Carlisle Indian School, which existed in mid-Pennsylvania between the Indian wars of the eighteen-seventies and World War I, was a curious institution. As Mary described the place, it seemed to have been designed to civilize Indian youth by forcibly thrusting them into the white man's mould. Everything Indian: speech, gestures, clothing, food habits, religion and miscellaneous customs must be laid aside, and entirely replaced with its white equivalent. Set down coldly the process sounds brutally harsh. Actually it must have been worked with kindness, for Mary had loved the place and everything connected with it. She had stayed on the campus or in its vicinity from girlhood to young womanhood, and still spoke longingly of it.

In part her devotion must have sprung from the fact that she came from a world where individual discipline for the general good was an integral part of the established order. In part it must have developed because the school offered her a stable floor in a world of insanely shifting social and economic values. But in greatest measure Mary's loyalty must have been due to the presence of members of the Society of

14

Friends on and near the campus, and to their influence on student life.

Carlisle School operated on "the outing system" which was invented there. For six months of the year the students attended classes, on a plan which our progressive educators would consider praiseworthy. A student was given employment in one of the school shops, where he was paid for his work. Not much, but enough to let him know that work had its rewards in the white man's world. If he worked in the school bakeshop, his vocabulary lessons were oriented towards the baking of bread and cakes, his arithmetic lessons centered around the computation of pounds of flour and cupsful of lard, and he might learn to write by inscribing A for Apple on the crusts of pies.

During the remaining six months, the student was placed in the home of a Friends' family, there to earn his board and keep either at specific jobs in the fields or house, or by doing miscellaneous tasks assigned to him by the family. He was paid for this work, too, but less than for the jobs he did at the school. He must learn that meals and beds had their worth, and that if he were fed more and better food than the school could provide at sixteen cents per day per pupil, he would correspondingly receive less money.

At no time during her period of schooling had Mary been allowed to go home. New children had been born into her family; her father had died; her entire tribe had been removed from one part of the country to another—it made no difference. Mary was in school at Carlisle, and in school at Carlisle she stayed until she was a woman grown and able to care for a home and family—a little matter of fifteen years.

The general Carlisle idea was that returned students should take back to their tribes the principles, moral, ethical, and economic, established and taught by the Quakers. They were to become the Indians of the Future, and, by precept and example, raise their tribes to their own lofty levels.

The plan might have worked had the students been able to talk to anybody but each other when they got home. However, their schooling had deliberately obliterated from their own minds the languages spoken by the Indians around them. Returned students spoke only English.

To the white people of the communities to which the students returned, Indians were Indians. They were to be dealt with at the business end of a gun or across the counter of a store, not otherwise. They were neither potential employees nor possible friends.

Returned students, then, were rejected by whites and Indians alike. If they defeated the purpose of their schooling and moved East again, they might find social tolerance, if not acceptance. If they tried to carry out the purpose that had been trained into them, though, and stay put and "uplift" their tribes, they led an unhappy existence, marginal to each group and accepted by neither.

Mary had come through the period of readjustment better than most women. She had taken her mother and her sister's orphan child into her home, so reestablishing direct contact with the Indian groups. She had married a man slightly older than herself, who worked at the agency as a carpenter. To the casual eye Mary's life was exactly in line with Carlisle precepts, and a telling argument in their favor. It was my fortune to witness the incident in which Mary defied all other standards to firmly establish her own.

At the time my study assignment was mapping. I needed to take my informant with me to identify geographical sites in the area. It was necessary to have a woman, and a woman who could stay away from home with a white for three or four nights in succession without dying of nostalgia for her tribe. Since Mary was already used to working with me, I suggested the plan to her.

Previously Mary and I had met on middle ground at the home of her sister. Now I drove directly to her own home, which the agency nurse had already described to me as "absolutely spotless."

But for all her spotlessness and Sears, Roebuck furniture, despite the first decent cup of coffee I had tasted since I left home, without regard to the frequent references to "Them" which were interspersed throughout our conversation, Mary proved to be thoroughly familiar with the countryside. She said that she was willing and free to make a trip with me— if I could go right away.

We left the next morning. Mary emerged from her house in a stiffly starched, spotlessly clean gingham dress; a kewpie doll grown fiftyish; round and smiling and pretty. Behind her on the porch stood the old woman and the little girl, smiling shyly and waving to both of us. Was I mistaken, or was there a faint air of relief about them?

I put the car in gear and drove downhill to the highway. The store stood diagonally across the intersection, and as we paused at the yellow warning sign opposite its door, the storekeeper appeared.

"Hey, Mary!" he called, waving an arm. "I was just coming to get you. Telephone! Long-distance call from the county seat!"

Mary shifted a little—just a little—as she sat beside me.

"Collect?" she inquired.

"Sure is."

"I ain't talking. Tell them I don't want to take no call."

"We've got plenty of time—" I began.

Mary shook her head. "I don't want to take no collect call. I know who it is."

This was, to me, a reversal of the usual attitude towards collect telephone calls. I might have refused a call if I hadn't known who it was, but probably not if I did. However, Mary's manner did not encourage questioning. Politely, ineluctably, she made it clear that the matter concerned was her business, not mine.

I bowed to the inevitable and switched the conversation. By what devil of curiosity I was possessed, I shall never know. But as a topic of general interest to women, and one on which I felt I could safely seek information, I inquired about the tribal institution of marriage "in the old days."

"In the old days," Mary pondered, "was about the same like always, I guess." Her English was usually beautifully enunciated, but many expressions and constructions she used must have been translated directly from her own language. Localisms flavored her speech, and occasionally she used an obscure, obsolescent word or phrase that must have survived from her days with "Them." "Men had lots of wives in the old days," she volunteered presently.

"How did the wives like that?" I queried.

"Oh, they like it," Mary assured me. "They got to like it. Husbands owned wives, like slaves, then. Women got to do what men tell them."

"Always? All the time?"

"All the time," Mary repeated firmly. "Wives is always weaker vessels, like the Bible says. Men got the right to run their wives, and the wives got to like it. Most of them thinks so till now."

"Was it their religion taught them that?" I persisted.

"Religion?" Mary just barely did not scoff. "Religion got nothing to do with it—in the old days. Religion was for men then. Women just went along, like always—like most of them does now."

The neatness of her distinction between the religious and the social left me temporarily speechless.

"I never paid much attention to the old religion when I was growing up," Mary continued. "Seemed like I was too busy around home. Mother kept all of us hopping, helping her make baskets. My father had a garden, and the missionaries had shown him how to work it, so we had to work with him sometimes. I just kept too busy to pay much mind to the way Indians worshiped. Then I was sent off to school when I was twelve and stayed there till I was eighteen. 'They' taught me about religion then, and I was just as happy being a Christian."

"Some people would say you were happier," I hazarded. "Did you ever try to interest your mother or husband in the Christian religion?"

"Oh, I talked to them 'bout it some. Seemed like Mother wasn't much interested. Those old people's religion—it's all right for them; makes them happy. They got their own stories—all same Bible stories. They tell how the Spirit Who Made Everything sent his son to live on the earth and teach the people. All same Jesus—all same God. Mother's happy and I'm happy; why should either of us try to make the other change?"

"Did 'They' teach you to think like that?"

Mary looked decidedly uneasy. She squirmed on the car seat, and she glanced apprehensively over her shoulder. " 'They' said that all the old ways was wrong," she said at last in a half whisper. "Everything. All wrong. 'They' said we had ought to give everything up, to live Christian lives."

"Well?" I demanded. "If that's what 'They' told you, why don't you try to make your mother give up the old ways?"

19

Again Mary squirmed—a childish gesture for a woman physically so mature. "It's wrong for me," she said at last, "but I reckon it's all right for her. And anyway, she's like Elmer—my husband—'bout some things. They're both of them pig-headed—set in their ways. They don't like nothing new."

There was a pause. Then Mary spoke, with a burst of confidence.

"Elmer's the one called me up at the store just now. He's real old fashioned, some ways. He thinks a woman ought to do anything he says, 'cause he says do it."

I waited, but apparently I was not to be trusted further with the details of Mary's family life. She shifted the conversation herself, this time, to a discussion of the points of interest we were passing and their tribal names.

Later in the day we reverted to the topic of wives and the treatment they received from their husbands. "Do white women always mind their men?" Mary asked me abruptly.

"Why, no," I said, thinking of some professorial families of my acquaintance. "Not always. Of course not. Most white people I know think that adults—grown-up people—ought to be able to work things out together, without anyone's minding anyone else."

"That's what they *think*," said Mary, setting an unerring finger on the essential point. "What do they *do*?"

I laughed; I had to. "I think it depends on the couple," I said. "The one who is stronger as a person usually controls the other, really."

"Man or woman?" Mary persisted.

"Man *or* woman." Then, because I really was curious about it, "What did 'They' say?"

" 'They' said like the Bible. The woman is the weaker vessel, and is subject to the man. But I think maybe you're right. A woman *can* be stronger than a man, sometimes. It depends on the man and depends on the woman."

The subject was closed, and therewith dismissed. Something unpleasant had happened in Mary's married life, it was obvious. What, I could only surmise. It must be something of a tragic nature, if it made her question the values she had acquired from "Them." Her questioning seemed more searching because it concerned one of the few points where "Their" beliefs coincided wtih the old Indian ones.

We spent the night in one of the small-town hotels that dotted the West twenty years ago. From looking at their signs, you knew how the lobbies would smell of dust and soapsuds and cuspidors and coffee, although never, under any circumstances, were those hotels equipped with coffee shops or dining rooms. This one provided us with two bedrooms with soot-streaked windows and a connecting bath. The sheets were gray, and the doors were provided with screens, across each of which was stretched a width of cretonne, thus, in a way, supplying privacy and ventilation simultaneously. We spent no more time in the hotel than we had to; we went to the pictures in the evening, and we made an early start the following morning.

Not until late afternoon of the second day, on the last lap of our trip, did either of us approach a personal topic again. We confined our attention to the business in hand, and I recorded place-names in such numbers that at times I almost suspected Mary of making them up. It crossed my mind that her inner revolt against "Them" might even extend that far.

Repeated questioning and back-tracking over the information previously recorded produced reassuring replies. Mary was not inventing, she was supplying genuine information, and I became ashamed of myself for questioning her integrity. Whatever her problems, she was not solving them by that escape.

We came in sight of the store, and I drew up before it, intending to purchase cigarettes. As we stopped, the storekeeper came to the door.

"Hi, Mary," he greeted her. "County seat's been calling you all day."

"Collect?" Mary demanded.

"No; you've got him softened up. He's paying for the call. Might as well get ready for your trip to town. He's expecting you." As Mary went inside the building, the man turned to me. "Can't help feeling sorry for that woman," he said. "Elmer's a good old scout, but he likes his monthly bat. He gets paid off on the thirtieth, and he comes in here to cash his check. Pays half on his bill—he's been in hock to me for I don't know how many years, and God alone knows if he'll ever get out—and then takes the rest of the money in cash and goes on into town with it. He buys a pint of liquor—there's always some saloonkeeper that'll bootleg to an Indian—and sits down in a vacant lot and drinks it. Then he goes back for another pint, and he keeps on doing that until he gets an urge to roam. Then he starts down the street, and naturally, the first policeman he meets arrests him because it's against the law for an Indian to be drunk. Then Elmer pastes the policeman one, and the policeman knocks Elmer out and takes him to jail. He wakes up sick and sorry, and starts phoning Mary. She borrows the money from me to pay off his fine, hitches a ride into town, and brings him home. He's back at work by the fifth, and they start all over again."

I pondered the situation. "What does Mary do for grocery money?" I asked.

"She picks up odd jobs, cleaning house for agency employees, or doing laundry—my wife says there isn't a white woman in the county can touch Mary's ironing. Now she has this job with you. If she can't get anything to do, I give her credit on the books for what she's got to have to feed the little girl and the old lady and eat herself. It's been going on for years now, regular as the end of the month rolls around. I'll never close out that account, but I'll never lose on it either."

The storekeeper's words made me think of the prices in the store. Merchandise there was five to ten cents higher than the same items in the chain stores in town, when I bought it, and prices were never marked on the articles. I had been there when an Indian shopped, and seen him pay a third more than I did for the same thing. The reason for the difference in price was abundantly clear—it cost the Indians money to finance the complicated bookkeeping their purchases required.

Inside the store, Mary's voice suddenly rose. Like many other people, she seemed intent on eliminating the telephone from her long-distance call. "Is that the jail? I want to talk to Elmer. Elmer. Elmer Many Feathers. You got him there."

A pause. I could hear Mary sigh in the silence. The storekeeper stood listening as intently as I did. Mary's calling back was a radical departure from established ritual. We were both curious to see what she had in mind; both sensed that something portended.

"Elmer?" The lady-like shriek cut across my thoughts. "This is Mary." The remark sounded unnecessary, but some people like to be told whom they are talking to. "Listen, Elmer. I been thinking." She was speaking rapidly now, intent on saying what she had to say before her courage weakened. "*I* did not make you get drunk. *I* did not make you hit the policeman. *I* did not make you bust up the furniture in the jail. *You* got in all that trouble yourself. You can get yourself out of it."

23

In the pause that followed, the storekeeper dropped on the bench beside his door. This was not only more than he had expected; it was more than he was prepared to accept. Mary's voice rose again.

"No, Elmer. I will *not* borrow the money to pay the fine. *I* did not make you get drunk. *I* did not make you hit the policeman. You got into this trouble; now you get out!"

Again a pause. The storekeeper wiped his forehead. I started to light a cigarette and found my hand shaking with excitement. We waited.

"I don't care, Elmer. Maybe a woman used to have to mind her man. But a man that gets drunk is a weak vessel, 'cause he can't even hold his liquor. I been thinking. It's up to the strongest one to make the decision. I decided. You can work out your fine, and then you can come home."

She hung up; we could hear the receiver snap against the hook of the wall phone. A moment later Mary emerged. She knew full well that we had listened, and her expression showed that she had expected us to do so. Revolt without an audience is a futile thing.

"Maybe 'They' wouldn't have liked a wife talking to her husband that-a-way," she stated in semi-defiance, "but 'They' never liked for anybody to get drunk, too." She shook out her skirt, still immaculate and stiffly starched despite two hot days of sitting in the car. "You pay Mr. Black whatever you owe me," she instructed me. " 'They' always said it was a weakness to get into debt. I'm going to get out of it as soon as I can."

Her head held high, Mary Many Feathers started up the hill towards home. Behind her she left the last vestige of the downtrodden Indian squaw, for she was a woman who had proved she could do her own thinking.

CHAPTER 3

MY MYSTERY STORY

WHENEVER today conversation turns to the supernatural, and my friends begin to tell of their personal, direct contacts with the Beyond, my mind goes back to my first summer of field work. I have gone over the episode so many times that my response has become automatic. Say "ghost story" to me, and I immediately remember my second field trip with Mary Many Feathers. Neither Mary nor I ever completely explained the episode—to ourselves, to one another, or to anyone else.

The day began normally enough. We set out together to compile place-names in Mary's tribal territory, as we had done before. Two weeks earlier, on our first expedition, we had gone south. This time I turned the car north. The shadow of the car was long and black across the flat golden valley that ran directly northward between two ranges of black hills. Here and there a point of rock jutted out across the valley floor.

25

It wasn't the colorful desert scenery that the travel bureaus try to sell you on, unless you considered the orange gold of the sunburnt grass colorful. After you had looked at it a while the orange lost its color, even in contrast with the lava black of the hills. The Hallowe'en color scheme was so sharply contrasted that the contrast presently vanished. The countryside became unbelievably monotonous. The dirt road over which I drove was tone-on-tone with the valley floor; a golden-drab earth line that stretched and curved and swung and stretched again ahead of us, as far as we could see. There was a round golden sun overhead, gilding a little the sheet metal sky.

"All this valley here," said Mary's tranquil voice beside me, "it belong one time to my people."

"To the whole tribe?" I asked briskly.

"Nooooo," said Mary, lingering as she sometimes did on a final vowel, "to my own people, to my fam'ly. My gran'pa was a big man one time, what whi' people call a chief. This was his valley, to take his people into it when he wanted to."

"Hunting?" I inquired. It seemed impossible that game could find any sort of hiding-place here, but one never knew.

"Sometimes hunting," Mary answered me, "but more times digging for roots. Us Indians didn't live sooooo much on fish and meat in them days. Camas-lily roots, water-lily roots, bull-rush roots; that's what them ole people like to live on. Them rocks all had names, those times, but some of them names got forgotten now."

"Try to remember, so you can tell me," I said, and Mary answered,

"Some I can tell. Some I don't know or can't remember. Some we aren't allowed to tell; names of magic places, they are."

26

"That point of rock, has it a name?" I nodded through the car window to my right.

"It has name," Mary told me. "It's called Wolf-Lying-Down because it's shaped that way."

I strained my eyes and could dimly discern that time, with wind and water for its chisels, had carved some semblance of hunched hindquarters; had set two sharp stones where they might suggest ears; had even added a tail curled along one flank.

"Why yes, it is a wolf!" I exclaimed. Mary beamed with pleasure at my response. The sun was higher, and its rays seemed aimed directly at us. "Mary," I asked, "are there springs anywhere along the valley? I brought a gallon thermos of water and a couple of quarts of cold tea, but the man at the store told me that sometimes in this weather car radiators dry out."

"Springs can go dry this time of year," Mary said gloomily. "It's a dry year, and springs don't hold out all through August in this kine weather. That's why the Indians go up along the rivers fishing then, when the roots gone anyway. But we don' have to worry. There's a store at the head of the valley. You get water there before we start back."

"That's all right," I said. "We'll look for the store and get some water there."

I relaxed, knowing that there was an answer to the first problem in even a temporary desert.

"What about the ridge there, Mary?" I queried after a short, comfortable silence.

"That name I can't tell you," Mary responded. "That's a magic place."

"How is it magic?"

I heard the rustle of Mary's starched cotton dress as she shifted her weight a little on the car seat. "In a good way,"

27

she said finally. "That's not magic that will hurt you, there, if you leave it alone. Some magics can come right down off them hills and doooo things to you, even if you don' bother them."

"Are there trees in the valley?" I asked presently. Early as it was, I was already thinking about lunch. Shade seemed a desirable accompaniment to the meal.

"There are trees," Mary answered matter-of-factly. "There's a place up ahead has trees. Indians call it Five Trees because there's a juniper and a mountain mahogany and a cottonwood and an elm and a wild plum there. 'Five' is magic for us Indians. Them trees grows round a spring, but mos'ly it goes dry in June. We can eat in the shade, though, when we get there."

"Is the store far from there?" I inquired.

"Store is 'bout five miles farther on," Mary said. "This road goes clear 'round the valley. You follow it from that place we goin' to eat, you go on pas' the store and then come home down the other side the valley."

"Will it take longer than coming back this way?"

"It take ten mile longer," Mary informed me, "but there's lots places on that side you got to write down."

"I don't really see how you can tell one from another," I said, gazing down the straightaway of the road. "It all looks like the same kind of country, and all exactly alike."

"Is all the same and is all different," Mary reminded me. "Is how you look at it, how you see."

"What about the place where the store is, Mary? Is that a magic place?"

Again I heard the rustle of Mary's dress, the slight shifting of her body in its place. But when I turned to look at her, I found her placid and her face was bland and innocent and blank.

28

"Some say it is," she answered slowly, after a considerable pause. "I don' know myself. 'They' tol' us there was no such thing as magic, an' I don' believe in it. It has a big rock point there behind the store, called Where-the-Black-Stones-Stand. Long time ago Indians use' to burn dead people there, so they don' come back and bother live ones. Couldn't bury them in the groun' 'cause they's too many rocks. An' they use' say spirits goes farther if they ride on smoke."

"Well," I said with an attempt at lightness that I didn't actually feel, "I suppose it could be haunted—maybe the spirits would come back to see if the fire had gone out, or something!"

"Some say they doooo," Mary calmly informed me. "I don' know for myself 'cause I don' believe in them. But the ole people say spirits can do loooots things."

Again there was a pause. Mary, beside me, seemed utterly relaxed. I concerned myself with the problem of why black rocks cast black shadows on the golden dust of the valley floor. Surely the shadows should have some other color in them. Mary broke into my reverie after a time. She leaned forward, and pointed at the roadside, to the right.

"There's a turn-off, up ahead," she said. "You see, goin' off to the right, that liiiiil road? That goes back to the Five Trees. You better turn there."

I could not at first make out the turn, but as we neared it, I could distinguish the side road, and a few minutes later I swung the car off to the east, back toward the black line of the hills. With the change in direction there was a corresponding change of light. The valley that had been golden dun before was dun without gold now; it suddenly became drab and colorless. We drove five miles to the foot of the escarpment, and there the road turned north again, taking us with it into a landscape that once again was golden.

29

Then the road seemed to dead-end against a point of rock ahead of us. As we came nearer we saw that the track had been cut in against the very foot of the volcanic wall, where it surrounded a small, basin-shaped hollow. Close against the rock there was a smaller depression, powdery dry now that summer had had its way with the land. The strange assortment of trees Mary had described grew against the further side of the hollow, backed against the rocks and away from the road. They shaded the earth without giving it coolness.

But we were grateful for what little shade there was, and rested in it for a little while when we had finished lunch. I brought my list of place-names up to the minute, and checked with Mary every landmark in the neighborhood. The information I was gathering that day seemed sparse, compared with what I had recorded on our previous trip, to the south.

"We've emptied both quarts of tea," I said at last, marveling at my own capacity, "and I'm still thirsty. I wonder how the car's doing."

I raised the hood, and plumbed the radiator with my finger. I stretched it as far as it would go, but my finger tip remained dry.

"I can't even feel the water, it's so far down," I reported to Mary. "I'll empty the thermos into the radiator, but I guess we'd better get to the store as fast as we can."

"Don' rush too much," Mary cautioned. "Maybe you dry the car out faster."

"Well, I could walk to the store from here if I had to, couldn't I?"

"Sure," said Mary, "you wait till night; you can walk it then. Not safe to now—this sun can make you sick in the head. Might make you think you see spirits!"

It is strange that the lack of something makes you conscious of it. We had spoken of water during the morning, but only casually. Now that I knew we had none for ourselves, and that the car, too, was in need, our thoughts dwelt on water to the exclusion of everything else.

"This time last year," I said as I started the engine, "I was swimming in a white-tiled pool. Where were you, Mary?"

"Me? I was fishing in the Klamath River and wading after my fish," said Mary, and we both laughed. "Don' get nervous an' scare'," she added reassuringly. "Bad things and bad spirits only come 'roun' when you get nervous."

"I'm perfectly calm," I protested. "Do you think the engine's all right, Mary? It sounds sort of funny to me."

"You jus' imagine it," said Mary, but I was not comforted. I gingerly traveled the five miles back to the corner, and then proceeded unhappily along the five miles of main road that separated us from the store. The sun had shifted again, and a dead, dull, and altogether desert brown country surrounded us. It did not cheer me up, although Mary seemed untroubled by it.

We saw the store ahead of us through the clear air, almost as soon as we turned the corner back onto the main road. A square, low, white doll's house at first, it grew into a little girl's white-frame, green-roofed playhouse as we neared it. When we stopped at the gate in the fence that surrounded its yard, the store had grown to the proportions of an incongruously New Englandish cottage, backed against the black lava monolith.

Inside the picket fence the desert had been made to bloom, as it can be whenever water touches its surface with sufficient generosity. There were pink petunias, as big as the flower-shaped dessert plates we used to have at home for ice cream. There were yard-long wands of gladiolas, bowed with

31

demi-tasse-sized blooms. There were calendulas as big as dahlias, and dahlias as big as football chrysanthemums. It was a mad garden, flinging its color against the monochrome of the desert as if brazenly determined to prove that there was still color in the world. In the middle of the riot there stood a reassuringly stolid bright-red hand pump.

I climbed out of the car into the staggering sun. I unlatched the gate in the fence, and started up a flag-stone path to the door of the store.

"Ask them if they sell us water," Mary called after me, and I nodded, remembering that in some parts of the world water was too precious to be lightly given away.

As I approached the door I had an uneasy suspicion—which I at first dismissed as the result of the sun—that all was not as it should be. Each forward step strengthened my feeling, whatever its cause. The door of the store was closed; that was understandable because many people close their doors to keep out early afternoon heat. The screen was also closed; that was commendable, for a tightly closed screen would discourage the flies that formed a shimmering living curtain over its surface from entering the building. No, to the eye everything seemed normal. It was my nose that was outraged.

The odor, sickeningly familiar and nauseatingly strange, seemed to wall me back tangibly from the door of the building. I stood with my handkerchief to my nose, trying to gather courage to walk through that offense to the greater one of the crawling, shrilling flies on the outside of the screen. As I stiffened my backbone and went forward, I remembered where I had smelled that smell before. It was in a country creamery, not too clean. There had been the rancid, heavy fumes of cream that had stood too long without souring.

And here before the door were the very same tin containers that had given off that odor—no, not quite the same. These were ice-cream containers. The cream had melted and spoiled, and generated enough inner force to dislodge the tightly fitted lids of the cans and spill a white and pink and brownish trickle over the doorstep. This was the source of the reek. Not spirits, just heat.

The stench of spoiled milk and the zinging of the flies seemed to hypnotize me. I could not return to the car, much as I wanted to flee to its shelter and the comfort of another human being. This place must be deserted; no one could tolerate such a smell for long. There was nothing that I could see to prevent me from going back and getting the thermos from the car, filling it at the pump, and then pouring the water into the radiator. But custom is strong and habit is stronger. I knew that I couldn't just help myself to other people's water without at least trying to get permission to do so. I held my breath, brushed a patch of flies away from the handle of the screen, slid through a crack onto the malodorous doorstep, and tried the door. It opened, and I stepped inside.

Inside, the place was a shambles. Shelves had been pulled from the walls and their planks lay helter-skelter in wreckage, heaped on cans of beans and corned beef and peas. A tin rack for bakery goods had been tossed askew, and the cakes and cookies and loaves of bread it should have held were strewn fan-wise across the floor before it. Bolts of yard goods had been yanked down from shelves still standing, and streamed frantically, defeated battle flags above the welter that had been the stock. Only a case on the counter stood erect and untouched, its inviolate spools of colored cotton threads a final, nightmare symbol that capped the rest of the horror.

A door in the wall that faced me opened, and a young woman came into the room. She was neat in a cotton house dress, fresh and clean and combed as any country woman would be at that time of the afternoon. Beside her, and holding her hand, came a little boy in a clean white sailor suit. And as those two cleared the doorway and stood looking at me, another woman entered.

She was dressed in black velvet; a long, full-skirted, cap-sleeved dinner dress that barely showed the toe tips of her silver sandals. Her fair hair—beautiful hair—was carefully dressed in soft rolls and curls. Her make-up was flawless; so exquisitely applied that at first it hardly seemed make-up at all. A second look showed it as a perfectly modeled mask behind which her face was hidden. Her hands were groomed; their nails were long and pointed and lacquered. Her presence, as she stepped before them, completely obliterated the other woman and the child.

"What can we do for you?" she asked me pleasantly.

"We're running low on water," I replied. "I'm afraid the radiator will go dry, and we're out of drinking water, too. I thought perhaps, since there was a store here, I could buy some." My astonishment was so great that my voice remained as businesslike as her own.

"We'll be glad to give you water," the woman in black velvet answered. We wouldn't care to sell water. We have plenty."

She reached beneath the counter and extracted a shiny tin bucket from the confusion. Then she led the way through the door and along another flag-stoned path to the red pump. Capably, without holding her dress out of the way and without splashing it, she filled the bucket and passed it to me. "Will this be enough?" she asked. "Come back and get more if it isn't."

34

The water splashed in rounds as large as the calendulas on the flag stones as I trod. I filled the radiator, and reached inside the car for the thermoses.

"You sick?" Mary demanded, when she saw my face. "It's the sun, I bet."

I set the thermos jars back in the car, and raised my head. It was a little swimmy from stooping, but there was no trace of the jarring headache, like a series of blows at the base of the skull, that I had been warned was the precursor of sunstroke. I shook my head and nothing happened except that my hair switched my ears.

"Mary," I ordered, "take the bucket back to the store and buy a spool of thread."

"You *are* sun struck," Mary declared. She clambered down. "You get in and rest a minute. Sure I take the bucket back."

I got in the car and leaned my head on the hot steering wheel for what seemed a long, long time. Then I felt the sag of the car as Mary subsided on the seat beside me. I turned my head to look at her. Clutched in her hand was a small paper sack, the right size to hold a single spool of thread.

"I saw it, too," she said in a hushed voice. "It was all there. I saw it."

"Even the woman in the evening dress?" I demanded, fumbling with the starter with my foot.

"Her, too," Mary said as we lurched forward down the road. "I saw her when she come out to the pump with you. She wasn't no spirit."

"Mary," I asked, "what do you suppose happened there? How did things get that way?"

"I don' know," Mary replied. She considered. "Nobody lives near there. Nobody within twenty miles. No lumber camps around; the harvest hands all done and gone home.

Them women is strangers to me. I never seen 'em before; never heard of 'em. And they ain't spirits. They real. Maybe the spirits didn' like 'em, is all I can think." She shook her head. "But you seen 'em—and 'They' always tol' us, there ain't no spirits."

CHAPTER 4

A FEW DEFINITIONS

A LONG time ago I learned that most books are written backwards, and are often read in the same way. Most writers write their introductions last, and most readers read the introduction after the rest of the book.

Writing the introduction last is a convenience for the writer. It gives him an opportunity to summarize his material, and to provide his readers with what he considers necessary definitions, of his terms and of his point of view.

If introductions were always read first, especially the introductions to technical or otherwise specialized books, perhaps the readers would find such works easier and pleasanter to peruse. I have looked for ways to induce people to read introductions painlessly. One that has occurred to me since I began work on this book is to split up the introduction and insert it in the main text, in places where it seems likely that the factual information to be supplied would make the stories that follow clearer. I think I have now reached a point at which a few definitions should be introduced, and so, for your convenience, here they are.

Aside from the matter of convenience, there is another point. The chief aim of all science is definition and classification. This aim is a satisfactory thing. It is an excellent objective for science to possess, and the work toward it provides all of us with fine, stable pieces of information.

Science itself is best defined, from its Greek root, as knowledge. As knowledge proceeds from one definition to the next, it runs the risk of taking for granted or omitting essential points. It can even contradict itself. Just as you have firmly made up your mind that science means knowledge and knowledge means knowing, for instance, along comes psychiatry, calling itself *a* science, to inform you that knowledge is the sum-total of human experience, *known and unknown*. And there you have a definition that leads in the opposite direction from the concrete word—science—that you began with.

Science, you soon perceive, is subdivided in many ways. There are the physical sciences: geology and chemistry and physics, for example. There are the biological sciences: what we usually call biology, and physiology, and botany. There are what have come to be called the social sciences: history and sociology and educational psychology, among others.

The science which has absorbed me most of my adult life is anthropology, and it partakes in some degree of qualities from each group of sciences. Anthropology is a nice science to be preoccupied with, because it has a wide field of activities.

Anthropology defines itself, from its two Greek root words (*anthropos* and *logos*), as the *science of man*. That is what I mean by a wide field. Stop with me a moment and consider man—as abstractly as we men can—and you will

38

understand what a broad outlook an anthropologist can develop if he wants to.

In the first place, man is an animal. His prenatal development repeats, in an intricate and bewilderingly wonderful pattern, the history of the animal forms that preceded the *homo sapiens* we know. Observing the development of the human embryo, we can gain some perception of the long process through which *homo* became sapient.

In biological terminology, man is a vertebrate, because he has a backbone or interior spine. He is a biped because through painful, age-long experimentation he has learned to elevate his spine from its natural, comfortable, horizontal position, and to go about on his two original hind feet. This has allowed his former forepaws to develop quite different functions from those of locomotion.

Man is an anthropoid—a man-like animal. What a biologically *true* man would be, we still can only guess. We as yet incompletely developed men are lumped with our kin: the tree shrews, the monkeys, the baboons, and the great apes, in the single, inclusive biological group known as the anthropoidiae. We did not descend from monkeys. If we had, we would *be* monkeys. But we, and the monkeys tailed and tailless, and the dog-faced barking baboons, and the magnificent long-armed singing gibbons, all had once, too many millions of years ago for the time to be counted, a single common ancestor.

She was probably a tree-shrew, so small she could sit on the palm of your hand with her tail curled twice around your forefinger. She was one of the earliest omniverous animals to be created, for she ate fruit *and* meat in the form of bugs, which were the only animals smaller than herself that she could catch. Essentially, all her descendants in all directions share her diet to this day. Why her descendants parted

39

biological company, we still do not know. One child or another was a biological sport—in tree-shrew terminology, a freak—and he became the ancestral man.

Now it is plain to be seen that anthropology as the science of man has a direct link with biology. The branch of anthropology that concerns itself with human biology is called somatology, because *soma* means the body. Anthropology—the sum-total science of man—is a pie that is usually quartered, and somatology is the first slice.

Nature does not usually produce species out of a hat, finished and complete and ready to go, whatever the kind of animal. She plays around with an idea for centuries or probably for millenia, until she gets an animal or plant the way she wants it. She allows the species a brief period of florescence when it reaches its fullest development, and then she chucks it on the geological waste-heap, and starts in to perfect another kind of creature. This process is known as evolution in some states and it is against the law to teach it. That is unfortunate, because university students can seldom be kept entirely away from books, and even when professors are law-abiding and try to avoid disseminating illegal knowledge, the students somehow manage to find things out for themselves.

Not all of Nature's discards are preserved alive for the edification of later-comers as the *coelacanth* has been. A few manage to get themselves embedded in rocks of one sort or another, and become known eventually as fossils. That is true of *homo sapiens* as of all other animals, and so it has come about that there are human fossils to be studied by paleontologists. Many somatologists have begun as geologists. They started by studying all kinds of fossils, and gradually narrowed their field to the study of a single species— the rarest of all because it is extremely recent; the most fascinating of all because it is our own. So anthropology claims kinship to geology, and hence to all the other physical sciences, through its relationship to biology.

Anthropology's claim on the biological and physical sciences thus firmly grounded and clearly established, where do we go next? We go next to another definition, that of archaeology.

Archaeology is the Greek name for the study of *man of the past*, but that definition, which could easily include fossil man, is far too broad. Archaeology is, more specifically, the study of the past *cultures of man.*

That word *culture* is going to turn up so often from this point on that its definition deserves its own paragraph. In the anthropological sense, culture does not mean listening to the symphony broadcasts on Sunday afternoons, or subscribing to the Book-Every-So-Often Club, or keeping the plumbing indoors. Nor does it mean something that you preserve on ice and look at through a microscope. On the other hand, it can and does include all these things and many more.

Culture to an anthropologist is: The sum-total of the habits, beliefs, arts, skills, speech, customs, traditions, mores, and knowledge of *man as a member of a society.* An individual biological specimen of humanity cannot have an anthropological culture until he is joined by someone else. Then the two comprise a society and a culture begins. Adam alone in the Garden was uncultured, but the moment Eve appeared a culture started.

Archaeology, then, is the second major division of anthropology. It is related on the one hand to geology, for archaeological specimens are usually buried and therefore on their way to becoming fossils. Archaeology is also related to history, for history begins where archaeology stops. Actually the dividing-line between them is so thin, so blurred, that sometimes it completely disappears.

Through history archaeology is related to the social sciences, and here we enter a field of controversy compared to which the Battle of the Bulge was an afternoon stroll. Is— can—a social study be scientific?

The social scientist says "Yes," and rests his claim on the definition of science with which we began. Science means knowledge, he says, and the knowledge of society and its workings is consequently a science. The physical and biological scientists, on the other hand, insist that to them science means knowledge in terms of ponderables—weights and measures and concrete comparisons. You cannot be scientific, these scientists assert, about something as fluid, if not altogether intangible, as society.

Whether you agree with the social scientists or with their opponents, you can agree that society is a vast field of knowledge, capable and worthy of considerable study. Perhaps societies can some day be measured objectively—a day when the organization of some society makes available the scales needed for its measurement and comparison with others. Our own does not. We can only compare, and our comparisons are dangerous because we must compare with the eyes of the culture we know, and of which we are parts as it is a part of each of us. Our comparisons so far are subjective— hence, say all scientists, even the social ones, dangerously inadequate.

But to return to archaeology: Whether it is a science, as its adherents assert, or only a study, as its opponents are convinced, it is plain fascinating. I have never yet met a member of *homo sapiens* and of my own culture who could not easily be captured by the word "archaeology." Aside from a general tendency to confuse archaeology with geology, and to expect archaeologists to be entranced with fossil mammoth bones, most people know what archaeology is about.

Archaeology means, to most laymen, digging. You sink a hole in the ground, and out of it you take carved shells and painted pottery and what are often and unfortunately called "flint Indian heads"—usually quartzite knife blades or hide scrapers. You may also take out of another hole, if it is big enough, impressions of floor plans and post holes, and nothing else. Holes of the latter type are interesting only to archaeologists, and such holes never get into the newspapers. It's the buried treasure holes that get written up.

Archaeology makes its wide appeal to the general public on that precise basis. Out of nothing comes something—frequently something rare and beautiful and deserving of the museum case that ultimately enshrines it. You can see the specimen; if you are lucky and know the museum curator, you may even feel the object rest on your own palm. Its cold is the cold of buried ages, the spreading warmth that encompasses it is that of your own flesh. Nothing so brings death to life, nothing so short-circuits time, as this experience.

Out of archaeological holes in the ground also come dust colds and sprained ankles and dysentery from living in only comparatively sanitary conditions, and years and years of toil when the pieces are being put together. The public does not know about these things, or, if it learns, thinks of them in the same light as frozen toes in the Arctic or lion bites on the veldt. Romantic.

Almost everybody who visits an archaeological laboratory, and sees the artifacts—as most specimens are called—being restored, is reminded of a jig-saw puzzle, and says so. The artifacts are a jig-saw indeed, three-dimensional in its nature. Putting together the knowledge they can give, and turning the light that knowledge casts onto the present, takes archaeology out of this world and into a fourth dimension. The archaeologist who stops digging for a spot of theorizing often finds himself wandering into a void where time runs backward and forward, here and there, overlapping with space and turning on itself. If the archaeologist is a brave soul, he continues to theorize. But if he is not, he may run in terror from the bewilderment of possibilities, back to the safe certainties of his digging. Like the gentleman Voltaire wrote about, he cultivates his garden. Thus is the dirt archaeologist distinguished from the archaeologist of the arm chair.

For while archaeology implies antiquity, it does not always mean it. The archaeologist working in Europe or the Near East who interests himself in the Neolithic—or New Stone Age—goes back thousands and thousands of years, to Ur of the Chaldees, the Biblical city of Abraham the Patriarch, and beyond—far, far beyond. But an archaeologist working in either of the Americas may dig up Neolithic specimens that are less than two hundred years old—if he can be sure of his dating. The Neolithic ceased to be in the central United States in the early nineteenth century. It still exists, to some extent, in the Amazon Basin and in parts of Africa and Australia.

There is mystery in archaeology. There is romance. There is no way of totally defining the subject, or of drawing absolute border lines. Inevitably, imperceptibly, universally, archaeology merges with history and so with another major division of anthropology: Ethnology.

Just to make things harder, ethnology has two definitions. In some European universities, ethnology is defined as the study of living *races*, for it can be translated directly from the Greek as *the science of living man*. In the United States, ethnology is defined as the study of living *cultures*. There is a vast difference.

Race takes us back to physical anthropology, for race is a purely physical thing. The three great races of mankind today are distinguished from one another by skin color, hair texture, bone structure, and proportion of limb to trunk length, and by several minor biological characteristics.

The first of the three great races is the Negroid, which includes many of the inhabitants of Africa, and their descendants on other continents, the natives of Australia, and those of some of the Pacific Islands. These are people with brown-black skins, short curly to kinky hair, black eyes, and limbs that are long in proportion to the length of their trunks.

The second great race is the Mongoloid (not by any means to be confused with Mongolism, which is a type of idiocy that occurs in all races). The Mongoloid race includes most Asiatics, most Pacific Islanders, and all American Indians. These people have brown-to-yellow skins, straight, dense black hair, black eyes, and limbs that are short in proportion to the length of their trunks.

The third race is the Caucassoid, which includes most North Africans, most East Indians, and all Europeans or persons of European descent. These are the people sometimes called "white," although as a matter of fact their skins are reddish or yellowish. They have hair ranging in color from brown-black through brown-red to pale yellow. Their eye color varies widely, too, from brown-black to pale blue. Their limb-trunk proportions also vary considerably, but are most often intermediate.

Superficially, that covers the main racial divisions of modern mankind. It should be clear that the distinctions

45

among races have nothing to do with nationalities, languages, ways of handling knives and forks, legal systems, beliefs in the supernatural, religious rituals, poverty, or literacy. All these elements of culture overlap from race to race. All these culture traits are part of what an American-trained anthropologist means when he says enthnology.

Ethnology, as the study of living cultures, can be as simple or as complex as the individual student wishes it to be. An ethnologist of great ambition and determination and imagination might study the culture of the Twentieth Century Caucassoid United States, the most materially complex and least spiritually integrated the world has ever known. One with more modest aims could concentrate on the culture of a single facet of that life; say, the behavior and life patterns of students on a university campus, or the way in which fliers use their hands to give directional signals when they cannot hear each other speak. Or an ethnologist who is historically-minded can combine his ethnology with a handful of archaeology and study the culture of an American Indian tribe.

Do not be deceived by the apparent simplicity of that statement. A thorough ethnological study should include both the way a society operates, and the place within it of every individual member. The ethnologist should learn how the people he deals with reckon kinship—who are a man's relatives and who are not. He should learn how the individual member of the society regards each relative; those whom he treats with great and distant respect—sometimes so great that he does not even speak to them—and those with whom he is on familiar, joking terms. He should—notice, I said he *should*—learn how everything the individual owns or uses is made, and by whom, and its place in the house and in daily life. He should learn the religion, and observe (if he is

46

allowed to) all its ceremonies and rituals. He should learn the mythology behind the religion, and how to distinguish myths from the simple tales that are told for the amusement of adults or for the instruction of children.

It is a great help, particularly in handling mythology, if the ethnologist can learn the language of the people he is working with and its relation to other languages. If, however, he is an adult with a musically and linguistically untrained ear, he is seldom able to do so. The languages of many pre-literate (or, as they are sometimes called, "primitive"), groups of people are far more complex in structure and grammar than are the members of our own Indo-European language family.

Such high specialization is needed for the study of languages that linguists form a group apart, interested in the raw materials of ethnology only because they involve names and operative verbs. There are still many more languages in the world than there are linguists to study and analyze them. It is exacting, detailed, and patient work, and one who lacks the special genius required for it is wise not to attempt the task. The average, unspecialized person had best accept the linguists' pronouncements on languages.

The field ethnologist, without attempting the high hurdle of language, still strives for an ideal, and strives against sufficent odds. First he must "catch his hare," and the hares are elusive and are becoming increasingly scarce. Ideally, the ethnologist must find a group of people—of whatever race or nationality—that has not been studied before. Next best is a group that once was thoroughly studied at a time comfortably remote in the past. Then the present researcher's report can be compared with the previous one, and the changes in the group and its behavior over a given period of years can be noted and defined.

47

In the second place, ethnologists have to eat. They secure food by holding down jobs except in rare and wonderful cases. If you hold a job, at least a fair amount of time must be given to it, and if it is a job in a university or museum, as most ethnological positions are, that means nine to eleven months of the year must be devoted to teaching or specimen labeling. The golden dream of the ethnologist in average circumstances is a sabbatical year or a fellowship endowment. Sometimes these dreams are fulfilled, briefly.

So the average ethnologist has little time to give to original research, as he proudly calls his field work. Usually he has even less money than time; scrimpings and savings from his salary, or loans from fellowship funds. He drives an elderly car and he wears old clothes and he eats in greasy-spoon restaurants. All this is known as devotion to science, and it is highly commendable on paper or when somebody else does it. In practice it is less enticing, because ethnologists are human beings, too, with human needs and desires of their own.

Into his one or two or three summer months, though, the ethnologist packs an intensity of living and experience that are reward enough for the poor meals and beds, the loneliness for his own, the lack of books or music or relaxation of any kind that his discipline imposes. For that brief period he goes outside of and beyond himself, into the life of another people and, it may be, of another time.

But the ethnologist, in his plain humanity, can never leave his own culture entirely behind. That is his tragedy. Because his culture permits—to some extent encourages—the study of others, he can go where he goes and do what he does. The Roman legionaries stationed in Britain may have *wanted* to know something about the Picts on the other side of Hadrian's wall. Their culture did not permit them the knowl-

48

edge. To the true Roman, all peoples who were different from himself were barbarian inferiors, to be despised, not studied. In the culture of the twentieth century United States, all men are theoretically equal, and therefore one group is as worthy of being known and of being studied as another. Theoretically.

Thus, the ethnologist plunges himself into the life of a simpler pattern and a simpler age. So far as he may, he identifies himself with it. If he cannot make the identificaton, and find happiness in his cultivated schizophrenia, he rapidly ceases to be a field ethnologist and retreats to the arm-chair division of his science. There is room and place for both; there is a need for each.

But the true field man becomes for a time one with the people he studies. If they permit it, he lives in their houses and eats their food, whether he is comfortable or not, whether he likes the taste or not. He copies their gestures. He struggles with such elementals of their speech as counting and words of greeting. He sits through seemingly endless ceremonies in uncomfortable positions, with no relief for his backache. He gets mosquito-bitten and sun-burned and he takes notes until his fingers are numb and he must sacrifice sleep to transcription.

And he is supremely happy while he is doing it. He returns to his own world with a jerk of disbelief, and he spends many months shedding his laboriously acquired behavior patterns and reacculturating himself.

To what end? What is the *use* of ethnology? Or is there any?

For a long time it seemed that there was not. Ethnology, like speculative physics, long seemed to be a pure, or worthless in the practical sense, study. I remember when I was a graduate student I was shocked to my conventional roots

49

when a professor informed me that I was the kept woman of a tolerant, indulgent society. Only my own culture, he pointed out, could afford to support those who garnered knowledge solely for the sake of knowing.

The war of 1939–1945 changed that attitude in this country. Ethnologists found themselves in demand. Men in our armed forces were going into remote corners of the world, and only ethnologists could tell them what to expect and how to act when they got there. The Army and the Navy and the U.S. Marines supported ethnologists as they had never been supported before, solely to profit from the knowledge the ethnologists had devoted their lives to accumulating.

Nowadays it is conceded that there is a practical use for this once pure science, over and beyond its fascination for the scholar. We are men, and nothing that is human is unimportant to us. Our world is shrinking, yet with the shrinkage comes expansion of our information. Once only a few of us could consider the possibility of encountering Hottentots on their home grounds. Now the possibility is not too remote from the boy studying petroleum geology or the girl majoring in home economics. He or she may be sent to the Land Back of Beyond to show by precept and example how Hottentots can live in a mechanized world. We are a nation of missionaries; we are a people with a conscience. We want to spread the light of the gospel of the machine, and with it the light of the seismograph and the soy bean. Ethnologists are the people who can give others what we call the know-how to do so.

So the time has come for the world to know how these odd, once-ivory-towered beings live and work. Because I am one of them, I do not have to go beyond my own experience to show what happens when a twentieth century Caucassoid

American encounters a twentieth century Mongoloid fellow-countryman. Here are stories of how one woman has lived and worked and studied among American Indian tribes, and a little, a very little, of the great amount they have had to teach her and of the fragment of their knowledge she has tried to master.

CHAPTER 5

FIRST NIGHT OUT

No matter how often you have been shown how, or have done things in company with other people, the first attempt on your own is different. It's an exciting difference and a frightening difference, and is like no other emotional experience I know.

So it was with my first independent ethnological field trip. I was summoned to the office of the head of the department of anthropology one day during the fall semester, to be informed of my graduate-thesis assignment. Laboratory work was pushed into the background from that day on.

"There are two Indian tribes in the state that have not been adequately studied for more than forty years," the professor announced. "The Kiowa and the Arapaho. Take your choice."

I knew nothing of either group—for the obvious reason that there were only a few obscure reports that mentioned them in print. I hesitated, and, momentarily distracted, watched the professor's hand as it poised above the smoking rack on his desk. If he took up a pipe, it should be the Kiowa, if a cigarette, the Arapaho. He lifted the pipe and my future was decided. "Kiowa," I said.

"Very well," said the professor. He stuffed the pipe with thoughtful leisure. "When would you like to begin?"

"Any time," I declared with the blind confidence of ignorance.

The professor considered. "When you went on the fellowship assignment with the group last summer," he informed me, "all your expenses were paid by the foundation. What do you plan to use for money this time?"

I was flabbergasted. I knew the foundation had spent a large fund on the fellowship group, for my letter of notification had named the amount set aside for my individual research. I had nothing like it myself, and knew no one who had. Asking my parents was out of the question; they were as unlikely to produce spare funds for research as I was. My dismay must have shown on my face, for the professor grinned understandingly.

"Broke?" he queried. I nodded. "All graduate students are alike. Don't worry, the university can help out. Next summer we'll give you part of the department's research funds for the job. In the meantime, go on over to the library, and start reading. Anything you can find on the Kiowa or neighboring tribes. Take plenty of notes, so you won't have to burden your memory with what you read."

I went out of the office five inches above the ground, and floated airily across the quadrangle to the library. There I requested several titles at the reference desk, and subsided with them in a far corner of the reading room. I opened the top volume, but concentration was impossible. My own concerns were far more engrossing than anything that had ever been printed.

53

Library research seemed at that point a waste of time. Because, the summer before, under the direction of a man of experience and specialized knowledge, I had spent much time in learning how to approach Indian informants, how to begin and conduct and close interviews with them, I assumed that I knew all there was to know on the subject. I had learned, among other things, that I would probably remember most of the information relayed to me from an informant by way of our interpreter, but that it was better not to trust my memory, and to write down everything I heard. The one sentence that I forgot; the single, tiny, disregarded fact, might prove the clue to a maze of knowledge in which other researchers were groping.

Sitting there at the library table, with the piled reference books before me, I was sublimely sure that I knew all there would ever be to know about the technique of my chosen field. Nobody could tell me anything; there was nothing that I needed to be told. And the university in the person of the professor had clinched my certainty by decreeing that I was worthy to receive departmental research funds the following summer. I closed the book decisively. Everything written in it was second hand as far as I was concerned. My knowledge should come fresh and shiny new from the minds of my informants. *Then* I would correlate what I had discovered with the knowledge others had acquired before me. I strode from the library.

My decision was not allowed to endure. The next day the professor questioned me, with apparent idleness, as to what I had read. I acquainted him with my decision regarding original research. He shook his head kindly, took his hat in one hand and my elbow in the other, and escorted me across the quadrangle. At the door of the library, we parted. "You might as well waste your time reading reference books as knitting," the professor said cruelly as he left me. A wave of Argyle socks was sweeping across the campus that fall.

Meekly thereafter I read and made notes. I became engrossed in my reading, and my knitting became a housing project for moths. I was especially impressed with the work of one Doctor Mooney, who, fifty years before, had spent some time studying what I was beginning to think of as *my* tribe. He had written down his observations for publication by the Bureau of American Ethnology of the United States Government. The Bureau of American Ethnology, familiarly known in the profession as the B.A.E., had done what seemed to me an awful lot of dull, plodding, and entirely sound work on Indians during the previous eighty years.

Thanksgiving holidays were on their way. Football restlessness pervaded the campus atmosphere. Still I read, except for Saturday afternoons in the stadium. The student assistants in the reference room began to keep my books stacked under the counter, and to pass the volumes out automatically when they saw me coming. Again I was summoned to the professor's office.

"What are you planning to do over the Thanksgiving weekend?" he inquired.

"Go home, I guess," I replied. The Thanksgiving football game was being played out of the state that fall.

"Would you like to spend that weekend doing research?" the professor asked.

I weighed the known warmth and gaiety and friendliness of a home Thanksgiving in my mind against the lonely intangibles of present hard work and ultimate fame. Too long had the original research I yearned for been delayed. And I had read all the books thereto appertaining twice.

"Gosh," I said, "can I?"

"You can if you want to," my mentor declared. "The

budget allowed for an enlarger for the photo lab. I was able to get it on sale at half price. That leaves just enough to pay your expenses for a weekend if you're not too extravagant about Thanksgiving dinner."

"I don't want *any*," I gasped. "Just soup and a glass of milk—"

"That won't do," the professor said. "Eating properly is a matter of efficiency. Don't let me hear any more about this soup-and-a-glass-of-milk menu." He looked complacently at his own well-rounded middle. "Where would this department be if I indulged in such nonsense?" he demanded.

I shook my head. I was saved the problem of answering by the professor's next question.

"Can you shoot a revolver?"

"No," I replied. "I never tried to shoot anything but a shotgun, and I'm pretty bad at that."

"Get your coat," the professor ordered. "We're going out on the range, so you can learn what to do with a hand gun."

I got my coat, and followed him out to his car. From the glove compartment he removed a hideously ugly Colt .38. It was a small cannon, and the term "hand gun" was wantonly inappropriate for it.

The professor showed me how to break the gun open and make sure it was unloaded. Mutely and clumsily I obeyed instructions. By the time we reached the target range I had mastered the elements of having a hand gun in my possession.

The next hour was pure unshirted hell. I broke and loaded and fired and broke and unloaded and cleaned that Colt until I ached in places I had not know were included in the human female structure. I squinted and peered near sightedly; I supported my gun-holding arm with the other hand, and still my elbow bounced upward and the upper edge

56

of the target was the only place my bullets even approached. It became rapidly apparent that I was not, and never would be, an Annie Oakley.

"That's enough," said the professor finally. We returned to the car, and while he warmed the engine he regarded me thoughtfully.

"There's a Western superstition to the effect that any man without a gun can be scared by any woman with one," he finally said aloud to himself. "I think you'd better trade on that," he continued, turning to me.

Back in the office I cleaned the gun for the last time, and returned it to its owner. To my surprise he handed it back to me.

"Keep it in your lab locker," he instructed. "If you get a chance to practice again, you'd better take advantage of it. And *be sure* you take this with you on your field trip."

"Why?" I inquired. All this gun business was beginning to worry me a little. It also bored me.

"Don't you ever read the papers?" asked the head of the department.

"Why, yes," I replied, "I read the editorial pages and the comics, and the women's fashions—you said yourself in your lecture last semester that those were the things that truly showed the culture pattern of our contemporary America—"

The professor looked at me for a long time, and then, slowly, gently, he shook his head. "I mean the *front* page," he suggested. "The crime news, for instance?"

"Why, sometimes," I said. "A friend of mine had a burglary last week, and I've been watching for news about that. They took absolutely everything in the ice box except a leg of lamb—"

Again, almost mournfully, the professor shook his head

as he regarded me. "You bring to mind my own student days," he observed. "Freshman English, I remember, and that thing in Tennyson about 'My strength is as the strength of ten because my heart is pure . . .' You take that gun with you on your field trip, and if you need it, you *use* it."

The university was to close on Wednesday afternoon, the day before Thanksgiving. All my Wednesday classes were in the anthropology department. On Monday the professor summoned me to his office.

"We can get a car for you Wednesday morning, if you want to start then," he announced. I nodded mutely, rapturously.

"Now, just run over the steps you're going to take," he ordered. "Tell me, as if I'd heard anything else for the last week, what you are going to do when you leave here."

"Well," I began, "I go out of town on the south highway, cross the bridge, and turn west. I go through two small towns and one medium-sized one, and I follow the river road right along and into agency town, Anadarko, where the Indian Agency is."

"How are you going to recognize Anadarko when you get there?" the professor demanded.

"I'm not *that* dumb," I protested.

"No, but you have a certain absent mindedness about practical matters. Go on. How do you know when you get to the right town?"

"There's a sign at the city limits. I go into the town and to the main street, and turn right. Then I drive out to the edge of town, and the agency and the Indian school are there. I ask for the superintendent's office, and when I go in and meet him I tell him what I want."

"Why?"

"Because the superintendent is in authority there, and everywhere on the Indian lands in that jurisdiction. Nobody can do anything in connection with the Indians without his permission. He has jurisdiction over federal property and is federal guardian for some of the Indians, and his authority supersedes that of the state officers in his territory."

"Thank goodness you learned that thoroughly. You sound properly impressed by the superintendent. Are you?"

"Yes. After I get his permission I ask him to suggest people I can work with."

"He won't do that himself, remember. He'll turn you over to the school people, or the social worker, or the home-demonstration agent."

"All right. And when I get names and addresses and directions from them I go where they tell me to go and look up the Indians and go to work."

"I'm relieved to observe that you've got the general idea," the professor remarked. "Don't do anything until you've talked to the superintendent, follow all suggestions you get at the agency, no matter how silly or useless you think they are, and hunt up your Indians last of all. Don't be disappointed if they aren't just the kind of people you'd have chosen for yourself. This is only the entering wedge. You'll find the others later, if you stay with your tribe."

On the following day everything went as we had outlined it, with the exception of the weather. That was threatening and gusty. The dark blue that extended along the horizon at breakfast time gradually spread upward to the zenith. As the color spread it carried with it a bone-penetrating cold that pierced through my heaviest clothing, and made a mockery of the car heater. Clearly, a "blue norther," a phenomenon rightly dreaded by all plains dwellers, was breathing down the back of my neck. I parked the car before the agency office building as soon as I had dutifully consumed a nourishing lunch.

Inside, the building was stiflingly warm, temperature and humidity both being greatly increased by the pans of water that stood on top of the gas heaters. The superintendent proved to be friendly and cooperative, if slightly amused at the idea of there being any value in writing down "the stories those old Indians tell." He gave me permission to come and go on the jurisdiction as I pleased—providing I kept out of trouble and thereby occasioned none for him—and turned me over to the home-demonstration agent, a pleasant young woman, not too long out of college herself. In my excitement and enthusiasm, I forgot about the weather until just before I left the building.

The demonstration agent, having given me directions for finding an Indian family, whom she recommended as being "just like white people—really *nice*—" had accompanied me to the door of the office building. There we paused for a moment in farewell, and she glanced out through the pane of glass in the upper portion of the door.

"Have you ever driven on country roads before?" she asked, eyeing me doubtfully.

"I learned on them," I informed her, neglecting to mention that I had learned to drive only the previous summer, and in a time of drought.

"You'll be all right then—probably," she said, and opened the door, admitting a blast of cold air. "Remember, you can come back here and spend the night in the agency guest room after you've talked to the Camps and made your plans to work with them."

I thanked her, and departed. Walking down the path to the car, I leaned forward against the wind, as if I were diving

60

into the sleet that beat up out of nowhere to bruise my face. Once inside the car, I was sheltered from the physical battering, but the wind swept with a desolate wail around the car, half deafening me.

I started the motor, and while I waited for it to warm the heater, I remembered the Colt, lodged now in the glove compartment of the car. Here I was, about to approach my first Indian family entirely on my own. I could not—I would not—let them know that I came armed. That would be a dreadful thing. After all, I was plundering them of the knowledge of their generations. I could not do it at the point of a gun.

In my suitcase, behind the car seat, there was a box of cotton pads, intended for the removal of make-up. I knelt on the seat, leaned over its back, and took the box from my bag. I put it on the seat beside me, and opened the glove compartment, from which I removed the Colt. Having broken it, and made sure that my memory of its unloaded condition was correct, I stuffed the barrel of the gun with cotton, thrusting the pads in as tightly as I could force them with a pencil. I then restored the gun to the glove compartment, and got started.

The first three miles of my way led along the asphalt road. Then, following instructions, I turned left off the highway, and dipped onto a county road. This was one of the "section lines" that mark off the surfaces of the prairie states into a grid, each square a mile to a side. By driving three sections south on this county road I was to come to an intersecting line of the grid. A mile and a half—or a line and a half—east on that section line would bring me to the side road, really no more than a lane, leading into the Camps' place.

The county road was unsurfaced, but it had been recently graded. Also, a fact whose importance I did not realize at

61

that time, it was sandy. I went along it in second gear, cautious, but, on the whole, comfortable. I found the turn to the east, and took it. Immediately, the surface of the road turned from sand to clay, and the conduct of the car changed with it. From a vehicle that proceeded in a fairly orderly fashion and along a straight line, it became a vehicle possessed of a desire to proceed in any other manner. It slipped, it slid, it clawed at the crown of the road. It threatened to revolve.

I was frankly terrified, and forthwith I forgot everything I had learned about the management of a car. I clung to the wheel, and fought desperately to force the car to go where I wanted it to go, instead of allowing it to follow the line of the least resistance. I wanted to shift gears, but was too much occupied with the wheel to release a hand for that purpose. My feet trembled on and off the gas peddle and the clutch. At last, having reached a point where I could stand the slithering uncertainty no longer, I jammed my foot down hard on the brake.

To my intense astonishment, the car did not stop. Instead, it finally achieved its long-held ambition to revolve. The car spun like a top on the crest of the ruts that separated the road's surface. Then it slid, with a ballet dancer's litheness, through a long glissade to the left, and settled with a thud in the ditch. I sat parallel to the road, pointed in the way I wanted to continue, but with the car buried to its running boards in red, gluey mud.

Automatically I reached out and switched off the ignition. Then I sat for a moment, listening to the silence that surrounded me. Momentarily there was no wind. I was stuck, and I was helpless if I stayed where I was. Heaven alone knew when anyone else might venture along this nightmare road. The best thing for me to do was to get out and walk.

I shoved the door open and crawled out, to plow through the mud, wet to my knees before I even reached the road. I plodded along the ruts.

I had managed better than I knew; it was only a few feet to the turn-off into the Camp place. I turned up the lane, marked by parallel strands of barbed wire, but otherwise indistinguishable from the prairie on either hand. It was immediately clear to me that I could never have driven a car over this track; what I had been on was a golf fairway by comparison. It was now after three in the afternoon, and real snow was beginning to fall.

My head bowed to the storm I must face, my feet lead heavy with caked balls of mud, I plugged along. There was a house somewhere, I knew. I must keep going until I reached it. My world held no other certainties. Science and its obligations were forgotten. All that mattered now was shelter.

"Where you think you goin'?"

The voice startled me no less than the solid body with which I had collided. A man stood in the track before me, a square, brown-faced man, solemnly regarding me. Then, as he looked, the face split in two with a white, amazing grin. Without waiting for an answer, he took a coat he carried over his arm, and put it round me, over my own. He fastened the top button under my chin, took my arm, and piloted me the last hundred yards to the house, which was completely hidden from sight by the swirling white that blanketed the visible world.

The man opened the door of the house and led me into a kitchen. It was an enormous room, one side entirely occupied, it seemed to me, by the biggest wood range I had ever encountered. On the other side of the room, under a window, was a quilting frame. Three women bent industriously above it. An indefinite number of children and puppies rolled about the middle of the floor, in and out of chair legs, under and away from a long, oilcloth-covered table.

One of the women rose from the quilting frame. She, too, was an Indian; she, too, wasted no time on questions. She removed both coats from my shoulders; then, before I could stop her, knelt and jerked off my shoes. She departed through a door on the other side of the room, to return at once with a pair of moccasins which she thrust on my feet. In a series of snapping-quick gestures she snatched a chair from the table and set it before the stove, opened the oven door, and pushed me into the chair with my feet cosily toasting in the oven. She was a tiny woman—the top of her head came just to my shoulder—but she was so sudden in her movements, and so competent, that she handled me as if I were a child. She and the man exchanged a few words in their own language.

"I was looking for the Camps," I said when they had finished speaking.

"That's us," the man replied. "Your car go in the ditch? I thought a car was stuck out there; that's why I went out to see."

"Yes," I said.

"We get it out when snow stops." He grinned again. "Car all right when weather's good. When snow come, can't beat a ole mule." He surveyed me shrewdly, without antagonism. "You selling something?"

"No," I answered. "I come from the university. They sent me here from the agency."

"What you want?" he asked. He was not rude, just interested.

"I want to write a book about the Indians," I informed him.

"That good," he said, to my surprise. "What you want write?"

"Everything," I replied comprehensively, pulling my feet back to the edge of the oven door. "How they live, what they think, how they make things—"

He laughed, a warm, belly-shaking laugh. "You come to right place. You got lots time, too; this storm goin' to last three days maybe. Maybeso last a week. You ask us, we tell you. When we get tired talking you watch what my ole woman an' the girls do. You got pencil-paper?"

"In the car—" I began, and he laughed again.

"No good now. You got to use mine." Before I could speak again, he vanished in his turn through the inner door, to return with a red school tablet and a handful of pencils. Lifting a lid from the stove, he sharpened the pencils over the blaze with quick, sure strokes of a pocket knife. Then he handed them to me with the tablet. "Now," he said. "When you ready, we start writin' book about the Indians. Your hands work good yet?"

I sat and stared at him, and he saw my astonishment and answered it. "Long time now I been thinkin' somebody ought to write down ole Kiowa ways so these little young ones can know. I try, no good. I don' know English good enough. My daughter, she been to college, but she too busy social workin' for Indian Service; never got time to write for her ole dad. Now you come. We got plenty time, like in ole days, when was storm, people sit by fire and tell history stories from far-back times. We do that now."

He was dynamic. He was forceful. He was an answer to prayer. Just like a white man—perfectly nice—he might be to the home-demonstration agent. To me he was a power no more to be resisted than the storm outside. I forgot my mired car, the suitcase which contained my belongings, my

65

pencil-paper, and I forgot the Colt. Obediently, I flexed my fingers and opened the pad which had been thrust upon me.

"All right," I said, "where shall we begin?"

"You wait here," he ordered abruptly. "I got to get the record, make sure we go right when we talk." Again he departed into the other room.

While I waited for his return, I tried to decide what "record" he could mean. The women had placidly returned to their quilting; the children and the puppies frolicked around my feet. Nobody seemed to be surprised by what was going on; nobody seemed surprised when Mr. Camp reentered the room with an outsize volume, bound in shabby green cloth and stamped with dulled gold, in his arms.

"There," he announced, laying the volume on the table, "that's Mr. Mooney. He wrote about us Indians long time ago. Now when we don' know for sure what happen' we look him up in Mr. Mooney."

For a moment I wanted to protest, but I was still numb with cold and surprise, and the split second when I might have gained control of the situation passed me by. Meekly, I opened the tablet, and, guided by Messers Camp and Mooney, went to work.

All the rest of the afternoon I toiled. It was intoxicating; an informant who *wanted* to talk; who had his own ideas of what was and what was not important. At his behest I wrote and wrote and wrote. After dinner, when we were recharged with beef stew, canned corn, hot biscuits, potato salad, dried apple pie, and coffee, he wanted to start in again, but his wife stopped him.

"She too tired," she said. So instead of things to be recorded I listened that evening to the singing of Indian songs, accompanied by a drum made of a tin can and a piece of inner tube.

66

"Bed time," said Mrs. Camp. I looked at my watch. Eight-thirty. I knew I could never sleep if I went to bed at that hour. But she stood by the inner door, holding it open for me, and I followed her into a second room, through it, and down a hall. She opened another door, and turned to face me.

"This my stepdaughter's room. She away working," she said, and hesitated. "Maybeso it not good like you used to," she said. "Maybeso the bed not all right. Elizabeth, she got inner-spring mattress, she say is bes', but I don' know. Anyway, you tire', you res' good."

Mrs. Camp led the way into a room that had been furnished, I thought, by an interior decorator. Copies of *Vogue* and of *House and Garden* on a table gave me the clue to its daintiness and chic. The bed, which I examined under Mrs. Camp's watchful eye, was the best I had ever seen; I had never in my life slept in such luxury. Elizabeth's nightgown and robe, laid ready for me on a chair by the small coal heater, were of a quality I hoped to aspire to if I ever got a good job. I shed my tired clothes, got into the nightgown, and slid under the covers and between the linen sheets. There was a tap on the door, and it was opened in response to my call. Mrs. Camp came in carrying the most tremendous Navaho rug I had ever seen. "Only four blankets on that bed," she said dolefully. "Elizabeth don' like no more, but you might sleep col'. You better take this."

She laid the great textile over me, and, immobilized by its weight and warmth, I went perforce to sleep.

The cotton was still in the gun-barrel when I laid the Colt, atop a heap of scribbled tablets, on the professor's desk on Monday afternoon. While he bewilderedly examined his gun, I began to babble of my perfect Thanksgiving weekend.

CHAPTER 6

HOW TO GO ABOUT IT

Having decided that you will become an anthropologist, how do you go about it? How do you get started on a career in this field?

The academic steps are reasonably simple. You elect your major, and with the guidance of your professors enroll in courses in anthropology and its related fields. If you plan on somatology as a life work, you may study biology, physiology, anatomy—in fact, somatologists often take full pre-medical courses. Most of them also take courses in paleontology, and some add statistical training to their other work.

A knowledge of human biology is useful also to the archaeologist. To it he usually adds some work in the fields of history and sociology, a few basic courses in paleontology, and a smattering of structural geology. If he has time, he may also study the histories of art and architecture.

The ethnologist needs all these disciplines and more. His training is generally heavily weighted on the historical and sociological side, but he needs all the information on human biology and geography that he can soak up. He can also use a fund of information on costume history, music, primitive drama, world literature, languages and phonetics (if he has the slightest aptitude for either), auto mechanics, camp cookery, elemental hygiene, diet and its effect on the average body, trade goods from the time of the Phoenicians until the most recent importations from Occupied Japan, and etiquette.

If he can whip up a minor enthusiasm for economic botany, and preserve the fragments of a sense of humor and an interest in everyday human activities, the ethnologist is set to go into the field. Naturally, a smattering of information about photography will come in handy when he gets there, and cartography is never to be despised as a tool.

In other words, the ethnologist, who is properly occupied with the activities of living man as a member of a living society, can afford to ignore none of the factors which make any living man what he has become. Nor can he be ignorant of the amount of time consumed in the process. Nor—since it is a part of culture—of what end the living man holds in view as his ultimate goal.

I always start my formal interviews with the subject of etiquette. Etiquette has several advantages as a topic of conversation. In the first place, any informant can see with half an eye that you are a stranger. The color of your skin and hair, your clothing, the language you speak and the one you don't speak, your gestures or lack of them—all mark you as an outsider. The informant, being an adult of normal intelligence, has encountered other strangers on previous occasions, and he knows already that their ways are as foreign to his as their appearance.

Since there is no known method by which either of you

can persuade the other that your backgrounds or experiences or trainings are similar, the best thing to do is to turn this potential liability into an asset. Be frank about it. Walk up to your informant, and say, as directly as your own nature allows:

"I am a stranger here. I am ignorant. Through ignorance, I may break rules that your children know enough to respect. Will you help me to observe the rules by telling me what they are? In that way, I can avoid seeming rude or hurting peoples' feelings. I don't want anyone to think of me as a mannerless person. But I may seem to be one if you do not tell me what good manners are."

This is the point at which you produce your notebook and pencil. Naturally, if you are to remember all the fine points of polite behavior, you will have to write them down for quick and ready reference. The notebook and pencil have been in evidence as part of your clothing ever since you first appeared, but this is the first time they have been put to use.

It is amazing the amount of information, and leads to other kinds of information, that now go into the notebook. First, of course, the date and place. And then, "Is it polite for me to ask you your name?"

Our culture initiates polite social relationships by introducing people by name, but that is not a universal practice. As a matter of fact, in many parts of the world to speak a person's given name is to be shockingly rude. His name is a part of himself—how many of us own monogrammed handkerchiefs?—and it may well be the most sacred and secret portion of his personality. In fact, it is not impossible for a man to have a nickname—literally, a handle—which he gives you to take hold of him by, but which is not his *name* at all. It is what he is *called*. Behind the nickname will be another nickname which his family uses. No one else with any pretensions to good manners would think of employing it.

Behind the family name may be a third—the man's real name—which is so sacred that even he himself does not know it. Only the priest who gave it to him, and perhaps one of his parents, will have any idea at all what his real name is. He may prefer to be called by a term which is not anybody's name, but which denotes his status in his group, his relationship to another person, or his age.

So you inquire of your new acquaintance if it is polite for you to ask his name, and you put down in your notebook, not only his exact words, but, if you can, how he looked and acted when he spoke. Did his eyes meet yours, or did he glance away? Was he nervous or self-assured? Did he make any gesture towards or away from you as he spoke?

The question of the tape recorder is sure to come up, and this is a good place to deal with it. I have never used one, for several reasons. First, I got started on ethnological field work before there were any tape recorders. Second, since I make a point of working with informants on their home grounds instead of bringing them to mine, I am often in places where there are no electric outlets to plug the tape recorder into. Third, as a general rule, the best informants are elderly people. It is an emotional strain for them to talk to a stranger at the best of times. To talk in front of a whirling mechanical gadget could be impossible for them. Fourth, I have never had that much ready cash available when there was a tape recorder to be bought, and, fifth, being mechanically inept even with gross articles like automobiles, I would probably wreck a delicate piece of machinery the first time I tried to use it.

Tape recorders undoubtedly have their place in the ethnological world. They are invaluable for recording songs, and I have friends who use them by the hour with specially

trained informants, in making records of spoken mythological texts. Recorders are excellent for preserving all sorts
of linguistic information. But I imagine that both the
ethnologist and the informant must go through a prolonged
training process before being able to use a recorder to the
best advantage. And since the material recorded by the
machine must ultimately be transcribed anyway, I stick to
the old familiar notebook and pencil.

Only when your informant tells you whether or not he may
speak his name for your ears do you tell him yours. You can
always tell where you came from and why, of course, and I
am assuming that you have already done so. But be careful
with your name. And, at first, give it formally. You're asking
about good manners, aren't you? Do complete strangers in
your own culture call you Bill or Kate? Give your name as
Mr. Little or Miss York. Later, especially if the name is
difficult for him to pronounce, your informant may ask you
if you have another one. Then, if you have become friends,
tell him about William or Katherine. Later still, as you become increasingly intimate, you may substitute Bill or Kate.
But don't dash into first names the very morning you meet
the man.

This apparently simple exchange of names, and the
writing down of the pertinent information attached to it,
may consume most of a morning. That is not surprising. You
are both uneasy, consequently tense, therefore not talking
freely. Your own back is aching, and your new acquaintance
is beginning to droop. This is the time for a cigarette, or for
a cup of coffee from the thermos in your car. Either break is
going to produce further information, to be jotted down
forthwith. After all, you will both have to get accustomed to
the use, as well as to the presence, of the notebook and
pencil.

Either your informant smokes or he doesn't. If he does, the way in which he accepts the cigarette, holds it, tamps it or doesn't, and handles a match, are all indicative both of familiar motion patterns and of sacred numbers in his culture. Three on a match, remember? How many people do you know who smack a cigarette on wrist or chair arm or palm three times before lighting it?

If the informant doesn't smoke, the field may be even more fertile. As soon as he *doesn't* do anything, you may be encountering a tabu. Do *not*, at this present moment when each of you is feeling his way, ask him why he doesn't smoke. Just record the simple fact, along with any statement he may volunteer to accompany it: He has a cold, tobacco doesn't agree with him, he isn't allowed to, he just put one out. If you are a woman, or if your informant is a woman, you must be especially careful. The questions of whether women may smoke at all—if so, what women, when, where, and under what circumstances—preoccupy many other societies as much as they do our own.

The cup of coffee can be just as rewarding. Acceptance or rejection of coffee or cream or sugar may indicate presence or absence of dietary tabus as well as personal preference. Who is served first—older or younger person, man or woman, host or guest? Put the facts down, and with them, once again, *any* voluntary accompanying statements.

Now you have both relaxed a little, and you are ready to go back to work. Here is where you get in a plug for yourself. You indicate that you would like to come back the next day. May you? Permission given, you ask how to behave when you return. Shall you knock on a door, or should you stand at a distance from the dwelling and call to those within, approaching no nearer until they have given you permission to do so? If you knock, how shall you do it? With your finger tips, your knuckles, or your elbows? If your arms are full, is it allowable to kick the door gently with the toe of one shoe or the other? Or with a heel? (This is an important thing to find out about. Some people consider it desperately unlucky—even a sign of death—to kick on a door.)

And here is another question that arises to plague all ethnologists, and that may as well be dealt with at the outset. Does your informant work as a free agent, or not? May he talk to you or not, as he himself decides? If not, whose permission must he request, and should you consult the same authority? If he tells you to consult somebody, rise as rapidly as politeness and your own bodily habit permit you to, and go and do it. Otherwise, this is where you stop, as far as getting any information worth having is concerned.

The morning has vanished by now. It is time, in any case, to get up and go home. If you stay for the noon meal, as you will probably be asked to do, you run into all the complicated assorted problems of table manners, and they are so multitudinous that it is advisable to know what they are in theory before you begin to practice them.

Besides, you and your informant are both more tired than you realize. At the moment you are enormously elated and stimulated, and you feel sure you could go on all afternoon, and thence continue all night. *Don't do it.* The great risk that you run in doing so is that your head and notebook become so crammed so soon that you feel you have learned immediately all that particular informant can tell you. Your knowledge is too casual and too superficial to be taken for granted in that manner. Don't wear yourself out; don't wear other people out. Leave, while you can do it easily.

One point still remains to be settled before you go. You know and the informant knows that you are asking him to give you during the course of a summer knowledge he has

acquired during the course of a lifetime. He has an investment in it, an investment in living, if nothing else. Therefore it behooves you to make sure he knows that you are not
motivated by a spirit of banditry. If you take, you will also
give. You explain that you know that with the time you are
taking out of his day, he might be doing something else.
Never mind whether you think he is physically incapable
of doing anything but sitting and talking. Assume that he
could; it is a compliment to his health and energy. Offer
him—in return for his time, *not in payment for his information*—whatever you have already learned to be the going
rate for day labor in that place and at that time.

Once in a while you will hear about informants who have
tried to hold up ethnologists, and who have demanded vast
sums in recompense for "just sitting and talking." They were
invariably people who wanted to be paid for supplying certain items of information. By their own assertions they were
in possession of certain facts and other people were not. In
my own experience, when and if those precious tidbits of
knowledge were disclosed, they were generally of minor importance to everyone else in the group, were freely available
from other oral sources, and often had already appeared in
print.

After all, in collecting information about any given human
group, the ethnologist is primarily concerned with the group,
and less directly with the individuals who compose it. It is
what the group as a whole accepts as a normal and complete
pattern of life that he wants to know about. The individual
who arrives at the evaluation of one portion of his culture
as of greater or less importance than another portion is an
aberrant individual from the scientific point of view.

It is just as well to distinguish, too, between the facts that
are of general significance and importance, and those which

may be strictly confidential on the one hand, or may degenerate into gossip on the other. That is why you ask about etiquette before you go on to discuss polygamy. Polygamy may exist within the group, and be accepted as an unremarkable type of family organization by all members, but it is best to be sure of your ground before you start on what may turn out to be a highly personal matter.

While you must always make allowance for the fact that information which has been strained through an individual mind before reaching you will retain some flavor of that mind, you are still most interested in what that individual *as a member of a specific group* considers normal, rational, and desirable behavior. And in as normal and desirable a manner as possible, you take your leave of him at the end of your first morning's conversation.

After lunch—and you may be surprised to find out how hungry you are—the best thing to do is to lie down. If your field of operations is in the southwestern part of the United States or any part of Latin America, where the siesta habit is firmly rooted, you might as well take a rest, because everyone else is doing it. If you are elsewhere, take it anyway. And then you can get up and start refreshed on the second portion of the day's work.

To begin with, you must transcribe your notes. Field notebooks are ephemeral things at best. They can get lost, or torn, or soiled beyond decipherment, or stolen—any number of tragic fates can befall them. So you want to get your notes out of the notebook and into some more permanent form as soon as you can.

How you go about preserving your information and making it available later, depends on you. There are as many filing systems as there are ethnologists. Some people like to use file cards, some like sheets of paper. There are those who incline to a chronological arrangement, those who prefer to file under names of informants, those who like topical heads and subheads. That's your problem, and you should solve it in your own way. But however you work out the solution, make sure of one thing. Adopt a single, consistent, workable system, and stick to it. And stick to it every day.

Daily transcription of your field notes gives you an unparalleled opportunity to review them. Now for the first time you see what your own omissions were, and what your informant left out. You can see where he evaded a direct answer, or deliberately switched a subject. You can observe how your questions started out in one direction, and when they began to head another way.

You may even find it helpful—I do—to make a series of questions on a sheet of the notebook, so that you will have a starting point the following morning. That approach gives everybody a pleasant feeling of continuity; of one day's work merging with the next, and of the work's proceeding apace, uninterrupted.

One of the greatest dangers to the ethnologist's peace of mind is his sense of the passage of time. It is next to excess of physical energy in the amount of harm it can do. The two together can be altogether destructive of the one thing you most want, which is a feeling of oneness with your informant.

Remember that it has been medically demonstrated that blood pressure, pulse rate, and even temperature are normally slightly lower among some human groups than among others. Remember that if you are a Caucassoid American you possess, probably, higher blood pressure, a faster pulse, and a very slightly higher temperature than many of the

77

other people in the world. Therefore, you go faster, wherever you go and whatever you do, than other peoples. It exhausts them to keep up with you.

Moreover, you have probably sought out the oldest people in your "contact group," and they tire more rapidly than younger people would. Their attention wanders sooner. They have more physical difficulties, in the way of stiff backs and rheumatic legs and rebellious kidneys, than people of your culture and your age group. They may be deaf or blind or crippled because of age and the diseases that accompany it. There are plenty of stories going the rounds about ethnologists who have killed off their informants by working at too great speed, and unfortunately some of the stories are true.

And then, while your informant may have all the rest of his life—much or little as it may prove to be—in which to think and talk about certain things, you have probably only a pitifully limited portion of time. Your physical make-up and the pattern of your culture impose speed upon you; your personal life pattern seems to make it even more imperative. In the human head before you are crammed the facts you must, you *must*, get—and there are game laws in our society which forbid the cracking of heads to extract information. So you are tempted to pound your informant with questions, with furious demands for information, regardless of all the unobserved behavior patterns that may be slipping by you in your haste. Remember, you would never question and cross-question in this way a person of your own society.

I did not originate the following rule. I received it from the first expert under whom I worked in the field. I pass it on to others for what it may be worth, for it has served me well:

Treat every informant, on each day that you work with him, as if he were the first person with whom you had ever worked in this manner, and this were your first day together. And treat him also as if he were the last living representative of his own culture, and you the sole survivor of yours.

So, returning to your day in the field, after you take a rest, you rise and transcribe your notes, and make further notes of other points still to be investigated. Then take any questions that remain in your own mind, and examine the literature on the group with which you are working.

There are very few societies left in the world on which *nothing* has been written. The information in print may be sparse and it may be scattered, but it is there, somewhere, if you have patience and ingenuity enough to hunt it down. Nothing will ever take the place of comparing the data you have gathered in the field with that collected by another observer from your own culture. Frequently the two sets of observations do not agree.

That does not mean that you and your informant are wrong, any more than it means that the other collector's informant misled him. Patterns of culture and behavior change; old ways drop out of use and new ones develop. Each form is valid in its own time and in its own way. The sex of the speaker and that of the person spoken to may also make a profound difference.

I am a woman and I talk to women; the last research on a tribe in which I am interested was done by a man working with men. Are they likely to have—or to have been able to —tell him what the women can tell me about childbearing and childrearing? Obviously not, and yet, for speaker and for person spoken to, one set of comments is as valid as the other. Nobody is misleading, nobody is being misled, and yet one body of information is radically different from the other.

At the same time, it is as absurd for me to expect the men

to speak freely to me about their ceremonial life as it would be for me to seek admission to a Masonic Temple. Nor will men be likely to tell me all about the way they conduct themselves on the war path, or about circumcision rituals from which their own women are excluded. Those things are none of my business; they belong to men only. I am beating my head against a wall if I try to force the men to talk about man-secrets to me as they would to another man.

So each job of work done, and each worker in the field, supplements and completes the labors of others, and that is why it is so desperately important that everything should be written down at once. What seems trivial to you may be the reverse to someone who examines your work in the light of his own interests at some future date.

And that is why I think the tape recorder alone will never be entirely satisfactory. It can catch words and nuances of intonation that the notebook cannot record fully, true enough. But it cannot catch the subtle shades of gesture, the lift of a brow or the turn of a wrist, that an observant eye can note and a quick hand jot down.

All this time I have written as if you and your informant were in direct communication. Unless you are a linguist or unusually lucky, that is seldom the case. The average ethnologist must rely on interpreters at least part of the time. More than rely. He is at the mercy of the interpreter, certainly in the beginning of his field research.

A good interpreter is one who repeats accurately, and with a minimum of his own emotional bias, what you say to the informant and what the informant says to you. A classic story of a bad interpeter is so old it is new, and yet it will bear repeating.

An old Indian was called into federal court, to be tried for beating his wife. And the judge asked him, through the

80

court interpreter, if he did beat his wife. The old Indian talked and talked, maybe for half an hour, maybe for a full hour. Finally after all that time, the interpreter turned around to the judge and reported, "Him say 'No.'"

Well, that's the kind of interpreter you don't want. Age and sex are relatively unimportant in interpreters; but there are certain qualities they must possess. A good intrepreter must have a feel for language *per se*; for your language and for his own, and for what one can bring to the other. And he must be friendly to you and friendly to the informant. You and your informant can afford an occasional brush at cross purposes; in fact, you can hardly avoid it. But the interpreter, as the person in the middle, must be the mediator between you, and he can only fulfill that function if he is on the best possible terms with each of you.

A good interpreter can sense when to lead an informant, and when to suggest questions to you. And he should—and if he *is* good he does—know when to keep his mouth shut and pretend not to understand one or the other or both other parties to an interview.

Most of all, a good interpreter must be indefatigable. He is the one person concerned who works all the time. Each of the others can rest while his words are being repeated. Not so the interpreter. He is the repeater; it is through his mind that the words and their meanings pass, and he must be tireless and constantly alert. A good interpreter is a gem beyond price. I have known three in my lifetime, and I prize them all as my sisters.

That is the interpreter for an ethnologist. The linguist needs an *informant* who has all the same qualities, plus a good sense of drama, and a fine singing voice. The linguist's informant is going to go from one language to the other, and in addition he will probably be used to record the texts of myths and legends, and also to record songs. Linguists' informants wear out soon and die young, as a rule.

But, all this time I have been talking about asking questions, and about how one question leads to another, as if question and answer were the normal way to go about this kind of work.

Not only is it not the normal way, it is not the best way. The best way is what has come to be known as the stream-of-consciousness method. Working by this system, the ethnologist at most suggests a topic of conversation. Thereafter the informant, with the ethnologist's pencil racing in panting pursuit, discusses the subject to what seems to him its logical conclusion. It may or may not appear logical to the ethnologist, but that is beside the point.

The chief objection to the stream-of-consciousness approach, and it is a genuine one, is that it takes control of the interview out of the hands of the interviewer, and bestows it upon the interviewee. If you have started to work with some specific project in mind, this can result in calamity. Say your chief field of research is the education of children. Without you to guide him, the informant may not stick to your point at all.

Instead, he may begin reasonably enough with his own childhood, wander off to what he ate for dinner on a particular day and how it was cooked and how it should have been cooked, announce that it should have been fed to a dog, bestow on you a few comments on the care and training of dogs, discuss cows and their relation to the family economy, and go from there to the life history of a cowboy he once knew in a wild-west show. While all these topics can ultimately be related to the education of children, the process of so relating them can be lengthy, exhausting, and discouraging.

Without a specific project, if you are in pursuit only of the general life pattern of an individual, the stream-of-consciousness method can be ideal. If all that comes is grist to your mill, topics and the order in which they are presented become less important. You will sort them out later to your own satisfaction, by means of heads and subheads and the filing system you have adopted. Meantime, you and your informant can have a huge good time "just sitting and talking."

Ultimately, this method of procedure can overlap with psychoanalysis. It carries with it the same dangers that an analysis would in inexpert hands. The informant delves deeper and deeper into his unconscious. Your relationship becomes increasingly intimate. You, as researcher, acquire a tremendous responsibility.

For you are taking from the interviewee something that is infinitely precious to each of us—the substance of his own identity. It rests in your hands to make him an equally valid, if equally intangible, return. Psychoanalysts call this process "transference," and it is the goal of the capable and conscientious analyst to restore the personality, intact, to its original owner.

Naturally, in such an intimate relationship, there are periods of strain and resentment. No normal human being can watch his personality being broken down before his eyes without feeling revolted and being filled with revolt. The informant can go through spells of hating you, and you should be alert enough to anticipate those periods. Those are the times when you go away altogether for a stated period of time, returning exactly on the day you promised to, or when you load the informant in your car and take him on a picnic or to a picture show. Those are the times when you offer small, unexpected presents, and little, unnoticeable courtesies. Above all, those are the times when you make no promises you cannot and do not fulfill.

The impact strikes in both directions. The intimacy may be too sudden and too intense for you to endure, and you may struggle to escape from it yourself. That is your problem. Resolve it as you can. Go away, read a book, turn on the radio, knit a pair of socks, go to the movies—do whatever you must for surcease. But remember this. If you go away and stay away, now, when something is too big for you to handle easily, you are through as a field ethnologist. If you once become afraid of your data or of your informant, you have automatically retired yourself to the arm-chair department.

All your accomplishment depends on your ability to detach yourself from your own culture. In fact, it is safe to say that you would not be where you are, doing what you are doing, if you easily found a satisfactory niche within your own culture. Mentally, emotionally, or in some other inner way you are a displaced person, or you would not have found interest in or satisfaction from the study of other cultures. That is your lack—or your great good fortune. Face it squarely, admit it honestly, take advantage of it if you can. Acknowledge it as a source of past conflicts, examine it as a possible solution for future ones. Can you live with your own remoteness, and even use it as a tool? Pass, brother ethnologist.

Only understanding, good will, and experience as you gain it can come to your rescue at the times when you and your informant are in conflict. *Your* friendship, *your* perception of small problems in relation to the great one of existence, and *your* generosity in interpretation are all you have to offer. It rests in your hands to make the return adequate. You cannot simply walk off to the halls of Academe at the end of the summer, leaving the loose ends of someone else's life stringing behind you.

For all these reasons, the stream-of-consciousness method is best left in the hands of mature ethnologists, with plenty of time to work in. Even some of them forever shy away from it.

In thus speaking of the difficulties of undertaking ethnological field work, I do not want to give the impression that there are only red lights along the road. There are plenty of go-ahead signals, too. But in the beginning you will inevitably be more conscious of the shalt-nots than of the shalls. I am only trying to save you time and grief by pointing out a few of them.

CHAPTER 7

ELIZABETH AND THE FAMILY ORGANIZATION

ELIZABETH became so much a part of the most exciting and absorbing years of my life; has been so close and dear a friend ever since, and always has been so meshed and intertwined with what I have believed and practiced professionally, that I find it hard to remember that there was a time when I didn't know her. To both of us our first encounter has come to have some unreality.

She was a name to me, and a name with pleasant associations, after the Thanksgiving weekend I spent with the Camp family while the university car was stuck in a muddy ditch. Almost from the moment that I laid eyes on them her brown, square, kindly father and her dynamic little stepmother were my friends. Our formal relations never began; we were on terms of joking intimacy immediately. That first night I wore Elizabeth's nightgown and slept in her bed.

On later weekends, when I returned at the Camps' invitation to help Mr. Camp write a book about his tribe, I continued to occupy Elizabeth's room. I read her books and magazines; I looked at her pictures on her walls. It was a strange kind of intimacy, and I began to feel that I knew Elizabeth very well indeed, although I was sure that she knew little or nothing about me.

Elizabeth was away from home at the time I became acquainted with her family, "social workin' for Indian Service," her parents always said, and I assumed that, like me, she was unmarried and a dedicated career woman. It therefore came as a considerable surprise when one evening Mrs. Camp lingering at bedtime to tell me goodnight, announced,

"Elizabeth say she goin' have a baby pretty soon."

"Oh," I said, "I didn't know she was married."

Mrs. Camp crossed the room and pulled a window curtain flat, then worked it back into its original draped swathes. "She married. She got married soon as she finish school. I tole her, I say, 'Elizabeth, you din't ought get married right off this-a-way. Woman work, she got no right to get married. You do poor job both ways.' But she say she want life like any other woman; she able to have it an' work too." Mrs. Camp regarded the window curtain with grim suspicion. "Now she fine out. Maybe woman with husban' can be social worker. Woman with baby sure can't."

"What's her husband like?" I inquired. I tried, unsuccessfully, to fit any man into the room I was occupying. It was entirely a woman's room.

Mrs. Camp recaptured a stray thread from the floor. "He all ri' I guess. I never meet him. When Elizabeth get married, we just could sell one calf; only one of us could go to the weddin'. So her dad wen'. Her own mother die when she li'l bitty thin', an' she was maybe fifteen an' away at school when her dad an' I get marry. So I don' know her so well, an' it seem' ri' her dad should go. He say this Jim is all ri' good man. Teaches math in Indian Service school. But they met while they was in college." She regarded me. "You sleepy. Good ni'." She went out.

I must have pondered the problems of married career women in general and of Elizabeth in particular for all of three minutes before I succumbed to sleep.

The next time I stayed with the Camp family I inquired about Elizabeth's health. I was spending alternate weekends with them now. My friends at the university said it was because only in the Indian home could I catch up on my sleep. It was true that I slept there as I had never slept before in my life. But sleep was the least of the attractions. Mr. Camp and I were coming along with our book at a great rate. I was sure of research funds for the following summer. Life had a wonderful, rosy glow that it shed on me from all sides.

Elizabeth was all right, her stepmother told me. She was able to work, and she expected to continue working until a month or so before the baby was born. She was badly needed, people with her kind of specialized training are never abundant, and Indian women in her profession are exceedingly rare. So her conscience made her continue on her job until the last possible moment.

I went home at the end of the spring semester and spent a week mending and letting out seams, and reading—reading for pleasure, not for information. It really did not seriously interrupt the continuity of my professional life, but by the time I started for the Camps' in the university car that was mine for the summer, I felt that I had been away from them for a long, long time. A lot of things could have happened in my absence.

A high porch ran around three sides of the house. It served as a kind of outlet area, onto which the activities of the household spilled whenever anybody had something to do that could be done outdoors.

On the porch, when I stopped the car beside its steps, a young woman stood at an ironing board. She was as square and brown as Mr. Camp, and her face looked as if it could smile as warmingly as his. Just now she was not smiling; her eyes were swollen and red as if she had cried for a long time, and her whole face was a mask of sadness. She turned and looked towards me and tried to smile, and could not quite manage it.

"You must be Elizabeth," I said, coming up the steps with my hand outstretched. "I've heard a lot about you. I've been looking forward to meeting you. How are you?"

Elizabeth put down the iron on its stand and faced me. Her palm brushed mine lightly, formally, as one woman of her tribe would, traditionally, greet another. "I lost my baby," she said.

"Oh!" I gasped. There was nothing for me to say, and I have since thanked Heaven that I did not make the mistake of trying to say it. Tears formed in the corners of Elizabeth's eyes and ran down her brown cheeks. I put my arms around her and tried to comfort her. Mr. Camp came out on the porch sometime later and found us there together. Elizabeth had stopped crying and was sitting on a bench, watching me finish the ironing and talking away normally about the university and campus life. I did not iron as well as she did, but I plugged away, and did my best.

"Well, what you know!" Mr. Camp greeted us. He beamed at me. "You got new informant?" he queried.

I beamed back. "Maybeso I take her for interpreter," I said.

Mr. Camp looked from Elizabeth on the bench to me at the ironing board. There was the beginning of a smile around the lower part of his daughter's face, although her eyes were still puffy and worn. Mr. Camp nodded.

"Maybeso you better hire her," he agreed. "I'm goin' away nex' week, an' I don' know jus' when I'll be back. Got to go on church business. I'm elder at the mission and delegate for this distric'. You take her for interpreter till I get back; then we see. I'm gettin' too ole to work all times if I can get my chil'ren to suppor' me." He turned to his daughter, and spoke for some minutes in Kiowa. Elizabeth listened, and then addressed me.

"He says," she began, and although neither of us could know it then, those words set the pattern for our conversations for the next four years, "he says that you need help with this work you are doing. He says it ought to be easy, because it is just sitting and talking. He says you want to work with the old people, and he thinks you ought to work with the old women, because they know a great deal that is going to be lost if you don't write it down."

"He's perfectly right," I said, struck, not for the first time, with Mr. Camp's perception and grasp of my object.

"And he says," Elizabeth continued, "that it is my duty to my people to help you. He says that a dishonest interpreter, or one who did not understand why you are doing what you are doing, could waste all your time and work and money."

"He's absolutely right," I again agreed.

"He usually is," his daughter remarked. "Well," she went on, "my husband has to teach in summer school, and my doctor won't let me do any regular work till fall. He said I needed a complete rest and change, and that I ought to get away from there and come home. Jim—that's my husband

90

—will be here weekends, but you wouldn't want to work then, would you?"

"Well," I said honestly, "I'd want to. But I expect I can find other things to do—typing and library research and things like that."

"Well, then, that would be all right," Elizabeth said. "When do you want to start?"

"Have you ever interpreted for anybody before?" I inquired.

"No," said Elizabeth. "Have you ever worked with an interpreter before?"

"No," I declared. "Do you think we ought to practice?"

Elizabeth produced a real smile. "Why not?" she demanded. "We've got our guinea pig right here." She addressed her father in a voice that was already slightly more formal than the tone she used in speaking to me. He listened for a moment, and then nodded briskly.

"He says," Elizabeth reported, "that he'll be glad to work out with us. He says why don't we all go out in the arbor where we can get away from the flies and be comfortable, and go to work?"

"All right," I said. I extinguished the gasoline iron and set it on its stand, and we all trailed across to the screened arbor at the side of the house and settled ourselves on its benches. Automatically I noted that the door of the arbor was on its east side, that cooking utensils and dishes were racked beside the old-fashioned icebox, next the kerosene stove, on the south or left of the door as one entered, ready for the family's summer occupancy. The arbor bench on the west, facing the entrance, had a comfortable, sloping back, and it was in its center that Mr. Camp established himself. He waved us to two lower, backless benches between his place and the cooking area. I opened my notebook and

91

jotted down the fact that that household orientation was unchanged since tipi-dwelling days. Then I waited while Mr. Camp spoke in his own language.

"He says," Elizabeth relayed, " 'What do you want to talk about?' "

"Is that exactly the way he said it?" I demanded.

Elizabeth nodded. "Just that way," she reported. "Of course, I can just give you the gist of what he says, if you'd rather."

"No," I exclaimed, "I want all of it, every single word, and literally translated."

My interpreter hesitated. She began to look worried and unhappy again. "I don't know whether I can do that," she said. "I'll try, naturally. But there are some things you just can't translate. They mean something English doesn't say. All I can do when we find one of those words is try to explain the idea. Is that all right?"

I considered the matter. I knew enough about French and German to realize that there are, indeed, some things that English doesn't say. "It's all right," I decided. "If you can give me the *spirit* of the thing—"

"I'll try," Elizabeth reiterated. She chirked up slightly.

Mr. Camp spoke firmly, didactically, from his place on the bench.

"He says," Elizabeth announced, " 'You girls quit chattering so much, and get down to work. We've none of us got all day just to go on talking.' " She listened to further words from her father. "He also says that if that's the way we're going to act, we had better get a woman informant, because no man will put up with it. What do you want him to talk about?"

Asking me to suggest a subject was a new departure for Mr. Camp. I was accustomed to arriving at the house and finding him primed with topics he was eager to discuss at considerable length. Never before had I had a chance to get a word in edgewise. As a result, many things that interested my informant had been thoroughly and even repeatedly explored, while the things that were of primary importance to me had been, I sometimes felt, slighted.

"Tell him I want to talk about the kinship system," I now instructed Elizabeth.

Mr. Camp closed his eyes and rocked back and forth on the bench, shaking with amusement like a laughing Buddha.

"He says," his daughter remarked when he had collected himself and spoken again, "do you know what you're getting into? Our tribe has all kinds of ways of listing relatives. We're kin to all kinds of people in all kinds of ways. He says it's so complicated he's never been sure he understood it himself."

"Well," I said, "if even he isn't sure about it, we'd better get it down on paper as fast as we can."

"You goin' to draw a picture of it?" Mr. Camp demanded, leaning forward, and forgetting in his eagerness that he was not supposed to speak English.

"It's the easiest way."

"Maybe we can work it out like that." He paused and reflected. "I tell you. You get biiiiiig sheets paper, so can make biiig picture. Then bring them out tomorrow morning, and we get to work." He laughed. "We better start early, 'cause this a long job, might take all day. You can't tell, we got so many kinfolks."

"Have you ever tried to work it out?" I asked Elizabeth.

"Goodness, no," she answered. "As Father says, it's very complicated. I'm not even sure how many generations are involved, or whether there's complete separation of sexes according to whether it's a man or woman speaking. I'm going to be interested in working it out myself. How about using sticks and stones, or something like that, and laying out a preliminary diagram on the table here? Nobody's using the arbor much, and it would be safe. Then you could copy it on a big sheet of paper as we went along, couldn't you?"

"You mean lay the family out on the table and play it like a game of Parcheesi?" I asked. "That's a wonderful idea. But let's not use sticks and stones; we might get mixed up. I'll get matches and beans. Red beans for men and white beans for women. Will that do?"

"Fine," said Elizabeth, and we all shook hands on it.

Since Elizabeth was at home and would need her room, it was tacitly agreed that I would find shelter elsewhere. I drove into the nearest country town, five miles away, and looked for housing. There was no hotel, but the town had a boardinghouse where the school teachers stayed in winter. The landlady agreed to take me in, since the teachers had all left on their vacations. And because it was summer and her garden was producing, her rates for lodging and meals were lower than those I had expected to pay Mrs. Camp if I stayed in Elizabeth's room.

All things were working together for my good. The less I paid for food and shelter, the more I could spend on informants and interpreters, and the longer I could make the summer's work last. I fared into a golden world and secured matches, red and white dried beans, and large sheets of brown wrapping paper at the town's general store.

There was a car with a government license plate parked at the curb when I left the store, and after a moment of squinting I recognized its driver. I crossed the sidewalk, to speak to that august authority, the agency superintendent. After a moment he remembered me.

"Oh, yes," he said when I told him my name, "you're the gal from the university who wants to write a book about Indians. How are you getting along? Find anybody to work with?"

"I'm doing just fine."

"Who are you working with?"

"The Camps, east of town."

"Oh, yes. Fine family. Good people, just like white people. Heard that daughter of theirs was home for the summer. Are you using her for your interpreter?"

"I certainly am."

"Well, fine, fine. I'll be out in the morning to see how you're getting along. Got to talk business with the old man." He laughed. "Imagine I'd better keep an eye on you, too. Can't have strangers wandering around, upsetting my jurisdiction." Since this was apparently meant to be a joke, and a not unfriendly one, I laughed with him. However, it didn't seem to me that the superintendent took his position or his relations with the Indians with quite the appropriate dignity.

"Come along," I invited him. "We're going to be working on kinship. It might interest you."

"Kinship, eh?" said the superintendent, suddenly serious. "Well, the Camps have plenty of that—and all kinds of it—all right. 'Bye." He started his car, backed away from the curb, and drove off.

By the time I reached the arbor at eight the next morning, I had forgotten all about the superintendent and his impending visit. Elizabeth and her father emerged from the house as I stopped the car—they must have been watching for it—and we all went into the arbor. Informant and interpreter took their assigned places, and I moved the cooking table from its place beside the door to the middle of the

95

floor. I opened my box of matches and emptied it on the table. I then dumped out two piles of beans, and heaped them, red and white, on either side of the stack of matches. Mr. Camp leaned forward, interestedly.

"Them your kinfolks?" he inquired. He beamed. "What you goin' to do with them kinfolks when we get done? Eat 'em?"

"I guess so," I answered absent-mindedly. I was spreading out the brown paper on which I intended to record the kinship diagram.

"You cannibal!" said Elizabeth. I looked across at her. She was smiling with genuine amusement. Her eyes looked better, less swollen, and far less red.

I picked up a red bean, and plunked it down in the middle of the table. "Tell your father, please," I said to Elizabeth, "that's he."

She did so.

I took a white bean, and laid it beside the red one. "That's Mrs. Camp."

"My mother or my stepmother?"

"Your mother, I guess. We'll begin with her."

"All right."

I laid a match between the two beans, the ends touching each of them, considered, and laid a second parallel match just below the first. "That shows they're married."

"Oh," Elizabeth observed, leaning forward, "you're going to use the University of Chicago type of diagram, then."

"It's standard," I reminded her.

"Oh, sure." She explained the proceeding to her father. I put a match from the bean that represented him pointing towards the upper edge of the table, and repeated the marriage symbol with two more beans.

"Those are his parents. The match going straight up and down shows descent."

"All right." She explained this step.

"Now, then. We can start with his brothers and sisters. I want their names—their English names and their Indian ones. And I want to know what he called them—the Indian words for father and mother and brother and sister."

Elizabeth reflected. "Some of them are dead."

"Does that make a difference?"

"He's not supposed to speak their names. I'll ask him, anyway. In the name of science."

Mr. Camp was leaning forward, as intent on the diagram as we were. He waved the query aside, before Elizabeth could repeat it.

"I'll speak their names," he said. "Got to, if we do this right." He addressed Elizabeth seriously in his own language, and she translated.

"He says it is very important to work this out," she told me. "He says he wishes he had known of this way of doing it before. It's dangerous if names get forgotten. He'll tell them all to you, and you be sure you get them all written down right."

With that, we went seriously to work. While Elizabeth and her father talked, I reproduced the diagram on my brown paper. Sometimes Mr. Camp was dissatisfied with my arrangements of the beans, and readjusted them to suit himself. For instance, he did not let me stop with his mother. His father had had several wives, and each of them must be included, with all their descendants, living and dead. We galloped through the sibling and parental generations, and stopped for a drink of water before we started on the grandparental and its increasing complexities. I straightened up

97

from the table and stretched. The superintendent was standing facing me, just outside the arbor, listening. He had apparently been standing there some time.

"Hi," he said when he saw I had noticed him. He came around to the door of the arbor and entered it informally, without knocking. "Hello, Camp. Hello, Miss Elizabeth. Heard you were home. What's going on here? Something I ought to know about?"

My informant looked at the white man gravely. "I think is," he proclaimed.

"You do?" the superintendent asked. "Well, what is it? Is she mistreating you?" He glanced at the table. "Got a new way of sprouting beans?"

"Got a new way of fixin' them," Mr. Camp said. The arbor was suddenly very still. Without knowing why, I withdrew from the table and joined Elizabeth on the bench on the south side. The superintendent bent over my diagram.

"I don't get it," he observed.

"You know that north forty?" Mr. Camp asked him.

"That forty-acre tract north of this place? Yes, I know it."

"*My* north forty," Mr. Camp corrected, with just sufficient emphasis.

"Maybe it's yours. That's what I came to talk to you about."

"It's mine. Them beans proves it. You see them red and whites there? Them's my dad and mother. That's me in the middle. That my brother that died—" Step by step, he led the superintendent through the mazes of the kinship diagram. He pointed out where names had been deliberately forgotten after death, and so lost. He pointed out where kinship terms had been used in preference to names, and, in consequence, two persons instead of one had been supposed to exist. He indicated the original holder of the govern-

98

ment grant to the north forty in question, the relationship of that person to himself, and how he was the sole surviving relative of the original owner, and, hence, legally and morally, entitled to the north forty. He went into the matter in concrete and satisfying detail, and Elizabeth and I sat on our bench and silently applauded him.

"There!" Mr. Camp said finally. "You see, I own that north forty. You got to assign it to me; issue me my title to it."

The superintendent looked at me. "Has he got it straight?"

I nodded breathlessly. "He certainly has."

"Have you made any record of this diagram?"

"Of course. Here it is." I spread the sheet of brown paper on the table before him and the superintendent studied it as intently as he had the bean layout.

"Would you swear to this in court?" he asked me finally.

"Of course I would. I followed every step he made. It's accurate."

"You may have to," the superintendent warned. "That north forty's part of a parcel of land the government lawyers have been trying to clear title on for the last five years. This chart will do it, and we may be able to work with it and avoid taking the case into court to get a condemnation of title. Can you make me a copy?"

"Yes," I said, "I'd—I'd love to!"

"Well, you do it tonight, and mail it to me at the office in the morning. We'll say I'm charging you that as a fee for working with these Indians. Matter of fact, I think you're getting off easy. There are going to be some mighty upset government lawyers when they see that chart. Good-bye."

He shook hands with each of us and departed. I stood, open-mouthed, staring after him. Behind me I heard a series of soprano and baritone chortles. I turned to see Elizabeth and her father doubled up with laughter on their benches.

"Oh," Elizabeth panted, "you looked so funny! So surprised, and so—I don't know—disappointed. You thought you were doing so well on a high, intellectual plane, and here it turns out you've been settling a law suit!"

"Elizabeth," said her father, shaking his head at her, "you don' ought to laugh at her. She's a real friend of the Indians. She done 'em more good than that lawyer I been payin' in town—and she pays us!" He rose, and solemnly shook my hand. "Don' you ever dare eat them kinfolks," he commanded. "We plan' 'em, maybeso they bring us up a crop more relatives an' we get some more north forties!"

CHAPTER 8

THE ADOPTION

THE first time an Indian adoption ceremony attracted my attention must have been when I was in my early teens. I read in a newspaper that President Calvin Coolidge had been made a member of the Sioux tribe. Accompanying the news item that day there was a photograph of the president, sheepish beneath an eagle-feathered war bonnet, and flanked by buckskin-clad Indians, either of whom would have made two Coolidges. Even to a juvenile eye the picture was funny, in a sad kind of way.

That was long before I had any idea of becoming an ethnologist; of having anything personal to do with Indians. Oh, there were Indians in Oklahoma where I lived, of course. The family next door was faintly Indian. The wife used to play the supposedly Indian melodies of S. Parkes Cadman on the pianola from time to time, by way, I suppose, of proof. I knew no more then of S. Parkes Cadman than I did of the Sioux or of their adoption ceremonies. I did know that my parents, rigidly classical in their musical tastes, objected violently to the pianola and to what they called its "war whoops."

Some time afterwards, when I was on my way to being an ethnologist and was directly concerned with the recording of American Indian manners and customs, I encountered adoptions into tribes again. This time the experience was intensely personal.

I went to work with a Plains Indian tribe, as "typically Indian" in the Hollywood manner as the photographed Sioux I still dimly recalled. These people I met had once worn buckskin, and a few families in the tribe still treasured heirloom garments of deerhide, to be worn in parades or to dances, and jealously guarded between celebrations. My new friends belonged to a tipi-living, horse-raising-and stealing culture; they had a slap-dash, good-natured, quick-tempered way with them, and their occasional moments of brooding reflection and religious thought were as ponderous as those of a medieval Celt. These were people whose religion centered on a search for a spiritual guardian, an idea not too far from that of the Holy Grail and its pursuit.

The life pattern of Plains Indian men had been, by the time I came along, recorded thoroughly by several compe-tent observers. The literature concerning the lives of Plains Indian women was less complete, and it seemed thoroughly natural and right for me to try to bring it up to date. After all, being a woman myself should give me a slight edge over the previous, masculine, field workers.

I was lucky when I secured Elizabeth as my interpreter. Getting a woman interpreter would not have been easy under ordinary circumstances. But the combination of Elizabeth's need for an outlet from her personal problems with my previous acquaintance with her family made our team work almost inevitable from the beginning.

When one added Elizabeth's background in sociology, and her thorough training in social work to the fact that she knew and liked the older members of the tribe, the wonder is that she did not do the research for me. She spoke my language and understood my point of view to an astonishing degree. She also spoke, and as nearly as I could tell flawlessly, the language of her own tribe. Withal she had a mind of marvelous flexibility, going from one tongue to another, from one pattern of language and thought to another, without strain and with complete idiomatic control of each. Even today I look on Elizabeth as the dream interpreter.

From Elizabeth to Elizabeth's grandmother was a single step. I wanted an old lady who could describe the life she had lived when she was growing up in the buffalo-hunting days. Elizabeth suggested her father's mother, and everybody was pleased when the three of us settled ourselves in the arbor by the kitchen door. Grandmother was introduced to the notebook and pencil that were an integral part of my costume, and induced to regard them as memory aids and not as menaces. She was amused by everything I did, and even more amused, as well as pleasantly excited, when she discovered that I was going to pay her for the time she spent telling me stories about "the old days."

Grandmother turned out to be an easy and willing informant. She liked to have a topic suggested at the beginning of a conversation; thereafter, she pursued it to the end, with a minimum of questioning. From time to time Elizabeth would interrupt the conversational flow by raising a hand, and would repeat to me in English what Grandmother had just said to her in Kiowa. I would write down her words, she would lower her hand, and Grandmother would continue from exactly the point where she left off, without, apparently, missing a beat or losing a thread from the train of thought.

We started to work as informant, interpreter, and recorder, but that relationship did not last long. Within a week or so we were entirely at ease together, and about the end of the second week Grandmother began to ask me questions about my own family.

Were my parents living, was the first of these. When I said they were, she followed with a seemingly endless series of questions about them. I was not the only person interested in the habits and customs of other peoples, as was soon apparent.

One question that recurred at frequent intervals and in many forms was whether my parents knew where I was and what I was doing. Repeatedly, I explained that they did. Grandmother required reassurance on the point. Weren't they worried about me when I was away from home? Weren't they afraid to have me spend so much time with Indians? Weren't they afraid to have me with Indians at all?

This was a question that amused me. I remembered my aunt writing from the family home in England to my father, at the time when we moved to Oklahoma City from Chicago, after the first World War. She had specifically asked, I now recollected, whether there were a strong stockade around the settlement to protect us from the attacks of the Redskins. I relayed this memory and it amused Elizabeth greatly. She repeated it to Grandmother, who laughed, but who also seemed concerned about it.

From time to time the old lady returned to the topic of my parents and their interest in my doings. While she was too polite to say so, she did imply that perhaps they should be

104

more informed about my goings on. Since for more than a month these had consisted principally of getting up at six in the morning, choking down a boarding-house breakfast of the dullest sort, working until daylight ended or exhaustion intervened, collapsing into bed after a boarding-house supper, and rising the next day to do it all over again, I hardly felt that I needed supervision, parental or otherwise. And yet, as time went on, Grandmother began to make a point of whether or not my own mother knew what I was up to.

This was especially noticeable after I adopted Elizabeth's name for the old lady, and began to speak of and to her—with her permission—as Grandmother. She herself struggled with my given name for a time, then gave it up and began to use an Indian word when she spoke to me.

"What does that mean?" I asked Elizabeth, the third or fourth time I heard it. I knew it was not the rather formal name, Story-Writing Woman, that Mr. Camp had given me shortly after we began to work together.

"That?" said Elizabeth. "Oh, that name. Oh, *that!*"

"Yes," I persisted. "What does it mean?"

Elizabeth hesitated momentarily. "It's the kind of name they give children if they're fond of them," she said warily.

"Well, what does it mean?" I needed this kind of information as much as any other, and I was determined to have it.

"It means Hummingbird," Elizabeth stated flatly.

"How nice!" I exclaimed. "That's a beautiful name. How do you think she came to pick it out?"

"Well," said Elizabeth, "she picked it because of two things. You've got red hair like a hummingbird's top knot, in the first place. Second place, you never keep still a minute. If you aren't writing, you're chewing on your pencil or wig-

105

gling around or scratching your head—your hands go, go like a hummingbird's wings, all the time, she says."

I was somewhat dashed by this explanation, but still I was pleased to have the more personal and descriptive name, after I thought things over in the quiet of my boarding-house room.

The Fourth of July was on its way, and with it a long weekend. My mother wrote to inquire if I were coming home for the holiday. In reply I told her that there would be an Indian dance on the Saturday, and with a sudden impulse added that it might be interesting for her and my father to come down and watch it. Why did they not spend the weekend with me?

To my surprise, they agreed to make the trip. They were both city people; I could hardly think of them away from pavements and their offices and the garden where they amused themselves with iris breeding and gold-fish raising. It was with considerable shock that I grasped the fact that their agreement to the trip meant that they were profoundly interested in and even curious about my present life. Grandmother was evidently right. They wanted to see what I was up to; wanted to inspect my surroundings; were willing to give up a comfortable and restful weekend at home by the fish pond, and to make a long and dusty trip by bus, in order to find out for themselves what the life ethnological was like.

I think it was the first time in my life that I thought of my parents as people, rather than as appendages to myself. Immediately I set about making the arrangements for their stay; inducing the boarding-house landlady to lend them her guest room for two nights, and to allow me to use her kitchen for breakfasts while she went away on a holiday fishing trip. I made sure that the raw materials for the breakfasts were available, including fresh cream for my father's coffee. I

106

found that I was quite excited over the plans for the visit.

Grandmother and Elizabeth, when I told them what was going to happen, were as much a-flutter as I was. Grandmother asked when and where the bus was coming in. I told her it would be late at night—eight o'clock in the evening— long past her bedtime. I intended to drive twenty miles to Agency Town, where the bus station was located, and collect my family. When could we be there—right there—in the arbor, she demanded. I informed her, through Elizabeth, that it could not be much before nine. She nodded portentously, and spoke.

"That's all right," Elizabeth told me. "She'll take a nap in the afternoon, if you'll let her off work, and we'll be here waiting for you when you get back with them."

I was puzzled by this suggestion of a reception committee. I was also a little uncertain why the reception should take place at what was for Grandmother the middle of the night. And I was reasonably sure that my mother and father would be more concerned with food and hot baths and with beds for the night than with being formally received.

Nevertheless, I met them at the bus station with the news that we were going to stop off and visit "my old lady" on our way to the bathtub. We could get a meal there in the county seat, and then drive past the house on our way to the smaller town where I had set up my headquarters. My father was more concerned with the present meal than with the eventual bath. "Where's the nearest decent place?" he demanded forthrightly.

We dined in the bus station on hamburgers and a fluid that had been used to clean out the coffee urn, before we proceeded to the car. Then, having stowed ourselves and the suitcases, we started out to visit Elizabeth and her family.

Light lingers along the earth of Oklahoma on summer

evenings. Daylight and dusk merge imperceptibly with one another and with dark. The sky turns by slightest degrees from turquoise to a Maxfield-Parish royal blue, and always, even on a starless night, misses being black. This was a night complete with stars and a thumbnail moon, all appearing with the suddenness of seasonal fireworks against the last sunset orange. The varied lights disappeared as soon as we left the town and its paved streets. That was a dust summer, and our small moving world was smothered and veiled and isolated in a curtain of red mist that traveled with us all our way.

The dust subsided like mist returning to a mountain stream, noiselessly, but so completely that it had the effect of sound, when I stopped the car before the Camps' house. We sat for a moment, watching the red swathing drop around us. I switched off the headlights, and dimly on our right we saw a spot of light—a lantern in the arbor. After a moment, the light rose a foot in the air and proceeded in our direction. Elizabeth was coming to meet us.

My mother stepped from the car and shook the dust from her once-crisp cotton suit. She reached mechanically upward, and adjusted her hat. She picked up her purse from the car seat. "Come along, dear," she said to me. "You'd better lead the way, and introduce us to your friends."

With my father treading deliberately behind her, she went forward to meet Elizabeth and the lantern. I performed the first introductions, formally, as I would at a graduate tea at the university.

Elizabeth in the lead, each of us holding another's hand, we walked the short distance to the arbor. There was a heaviness in the air that was more than the normal summer heat. This was a heaviness of anticipation, a nerve-clawing, tingling expectancy of the unknown, tightening the breath beneath the ribs. Why I, on comparatively familiar ground and surrounded by people I knew, should experience it, I could not have told. Or how I knew that it afflicted equally Elizabeth and my parents.

We came to the entrance of the arbor. Elizabeth held the lantern high, and motioned us to precede her. I moved ahead of my father and mother, and was the first to enter the door on the east side of the arbor.

Facing me, in the traditional place of honor, was Grandmother. She sat upright on the bench, her feet tucked under her and correctly turned to the left, the north side. Behind her hung a buffalo hide painted with geometric designs in red and black. I had heard of such objects, but had never before beheld one.

Grandmother wore a white buckskin dress and moccasins, instead of the nondescript printed calico I was used to seeing on her. Her hair was parted exactly, directly above the bridge of her nose. It no longer hung in braids—a style the missionaries had introduced some forty years before—but streamed aboriginally across her shoulders and down her back. A red spot was painted on each cheek; the bridge of her nose and a line down the middle of her chin were chrome yellow. Old silver earrings swung almost to her shoulders, and her arms were as heavy with silver bracelets as her hands were with rings.

On either side of her, with considerable space separating her from them, sat Elizabeth's parents. The rest of the family, in order of descending importance, were spaced along the bench. Nobody spoke when we came into the arbor; nobody moved; nobody but Grandmother looked at us. We stood, drooping and dust coated, in the light of the lantern, facing the dark-visaged circle, waiting for some clue to tell us what we were supposed to do next.

109

I suppose the silence that enveloped our entrance lasted considerably less than an hour; probably two or three minutes must have been the limit of its endurance. There was plenty of time for passages from the reference books I had read in preparation for this moment to course through my mind. I remembered that the tribe had once had an apparently well-deserved reputation for ingenuity in the invention of tortures. I remembered that the women were said to have been especially gifted in that line. And I remembered, incongruously, my aunt's phrase, from far-away, safe England: ". . . a good, strong stockade around the settlement, for protection against the Redskins." Then the mist cleared. Grandmother was speaking.

She spoke slowly and impressively, directly to Elizabeth, and when she finished, the interpreter turned to us.

"She's talking the old talk," she said to me by way of preface. "The way they do in a council or when there's something important going on. I don't know if I can interpret it; I don't get to hear that kind of speaking very often and it's different from our every-day way of talking. But I can try. It's not easy.

"She says,"—Elizabeth's voice and manner of speaking became more formal than usual—"that long ago, when she was a small girl, her people had barely heard of white people. They knew about the *Mexicanos*, who came up from the south to trade, and they saw that some of them had fair skins, but they never thought of them as a different people; only a different tribe. Then came the soldiers in blue uniforms, to build the fort. They spoke a different language from the *Mexicanos*, and they shouted. They had light hair and strange blue eyes, like water, shallow. They had see-far glasses and shoot-far guns that banged (that's the way she says it), and the Indians were afraid of them. After the soldiers came, the buffalo began to go away. Nobody knows to this day where they went.

"Then the farmers came. They looked like the soldiers and they shouted. They put fences around the land, so the Indians could only ride on the roads. The buffalo all went away—the last of them—and the Indians starved. All that she knew about white people when she was a little girl or a young woman coming up, was to be afraid of them." Elizabeth stopped speaking and waited. An answer was expected. I hardly knew what I could or should reply.

"Tell her," I said at last, "that these things are written in our history books. Our children learn about them. Now we are learning to be ashamed. Some of us are sorry. We would like to make up to the Indians for what we have done to them."

I stopped, and Elizabeth slowly repeated what I had said. A murmur ran around the arbor, men's voices and women's mingled together, with a sound like the wind shaking the leaves of the cottonwood trees down by the creek. I hoped that it was a murmur of approval, but I had no way of being sure. Grandmother spoke again.

This time Elizabeth turned to my mother, and spoke directly to her. "She says," she began, "that all her life she has been afraid of white people. All her life she has wondered what it would be like to know one of them. Then your daughter came. She is a young woman, and she has many things to learn. But she wants to learn them; she is willing to learn, and to learn from an old Indian woman. Nobody could be afraid of her—" Elizabeth's sidelong glance at me combined amusement and apology in equal parts "—and she is kind. She says—my grandmother says—that she has learned to love your daughter." The interpreter paused, and caught her breath. "I have, too," she added abruptly.

111

"I am glad," my mother said quietly. Again we waited while Grandmother spoke.

"She says," Elizabeth's measured voice resumed, "that her first child was a girl that died. It was in the winter that the smallpox first came to us." Mentally, mechanically, I recorded the date as one that could be checked when I got back to a reference library. "That child would be a woman older than my father now. If that girl had children, one of them would have been a daughter, your daughter's age."

"I see," my mother said.

"So, for that reason," Elizabeth continued, "my grandmother says she wants to adopt your daughter. She wants to take her for her own granddaughter, to replace the child that died and the children who died with her. But before she can do that, she must have your permission."

She waited; so did we all. My mother looked at my father, and he looked back at her and nodded. Then, without speaking, she crossed the arbor and took the old woman's hand. "Thank you," she said, and motioned me forward to meet my new grandmother and the other members of my new family.

That was my adoption into an Indian tribe. No war bonnet; not even an eagle feather. Only an offer, and its acceptance. No photographers, no record made except the one that I wrote down that night when, worn out with heat and dust and emotion, I reached the boarding house, and my parents were, I hoped, settled and asleep in the landlady's guest room.

CHAPTER 9

THOUGHT AND BELIEF

ARLY in my training, the professor of anthropology under whom I studied tried to impress upon me the importance of taking primitive religions at their own expressed values. "Don't compare or argue," he cautioned in a graduate seminar. "Remember that these people *believe* what they're telling you. Whether *you* believe something else or not is your business. Don't pester them with it. What they're saying is real to them, and you must never question its validity if you are to make a real study of their culture."

The professor neglected to mention, perhaps through excess of zeal, that such primitive groups as are left in the United States are unaccustomed to outsiders who refrain from the argument of religious questions. From the earliest conquerors, who abruptly hanged persons who disagreed with them on doctrinal points, to the missionaries of today who couch their arguments in social and economic terms, the American Indians have been exposed to a surprising

113

amount of theological dispute. That anyone should agree with them, or even listen willingly to what they had to say, was foreign to their experience with whites.

Therefore, when I first began to work with the Kiowas in western Oklahoma, and when I timidly suggested that I would like to hear about the religious practices of their buffalo-hunting days, I encountered silence. Polite silence, the kindly silence that greets a child who asks biological questions in mixed company, but silence. It was an all-obliterating blankness, one which did not deny me knowledge, did not even deny my right to ask questions, but did deny, totally, that answers to my questions had ever existed.

Elizabeth's personality did not help matters. Elizabeth had been away from her tribe during her formative years, first at a government school and later at a denominational college. Elizabeth's case-work training was overlaid with a theological frosting of her own, and she conscientiously practiced her religion. She was a charming companion, and no one, not the most suspicious white or Indian gossip, could ever say that Elizabeth was anything a young married woman should not be, in manner or behavior. She was a God-send to me in many ways, but there was one serious drawback to working with her. Elizabeth had her eyes open at all times for possible converts, and all her people knew it.

So whenever my car, distinguished from other aged knock-about cars by its university license plate, pulled up before a farm house, a brush arbor summer home, or one of the few remaining canvas tipis in the area, and Elizabeth climbed out, decorum immediately reigned over all who saw us. Conversation became correct to the point of being stilted, table manners became finical, and we were surrounded with an atmosphere of well-doing and good behavior that transfigured everyone around us.

114

This was not the atmosphere I wanted to encourage. I had left home and familiar university surroundings and come into the desolate blaze of this midsummer to observe people being themselves; doing what they wanted to do, not what they thought *I* wanted them to do. Above all, I wanted them to talk about what interested *them*, not about what was expected to interest *me*.

For weeks I was hopelessly disappointed. I tried all the standard approaches; sitting silent myself and waiting for voluntary statements that never were spoken; coaxing, wheedling, ignoring, direct questioning—and all to no avail. I returned to the university library and conned the volumes written on this tribe and its neighbors in the past—and had my efforts rewarded with eyestrain. I gathered fragments of information from the printed page and waved them under the noses of the oldest people I could discover. No information on the tribal religion was forthcoming.

"You ought to talk to my old uncle," Elizabeth remarked casually one day. "He knows all about those old-time grandmother gods, and the way they could make people obey them."

When she spoke we were on our way, swathed in the customary cloud of dust, to her grandmother's home. I was struggling to hold the car in the almost invisible ruts of the road, and intermittently watching the temperature gauge to see if the radiator had reached boiling point. As soon as it did we would have to stop wherever we were and wait for the temperature to drop—a matter sometimes of waiting from mid afternoon until sunset.

So I answered Elizabeth by saying, "Yes, we'll have to see him," and continued to deal as I might with present and material problems.

We three women worked together for several weeks. We

115

were all friendly and the atmosphere was relaxed; information flowed from Grandmother's lips to my notebook via Elizabeth in a stream. I recorded facts about the existence of women in that tribe that I had never seen in print, but whose authenticity I had no faintest reason to question.

And then I began to dream of tipis. They were usually hazy and were mixed with other dream elements, but they were recognizably tipis. I mentioned my dreams to Elizabeth and Grandmother one morning.

"Oh," said Elizabeth, as carelessly as I had spoken, "that must be because we all keep talking about them so much." I thoughtlessly agreed, and we continued to talk about tipis and the life that had been lived in them.

Why it did not enter my head to suggest to Elizabeth and Grandmother that in dreaming of tipis I might have had what their tribe called a power dream, I do not know. The literature on the area was full of references to "the power concept," as it was technically called, and I was by then thoroughly familiar with the idea. Power, I knew, underlay and transcended the tribal religion. Power, as the Plains Indians defined it, was the concentration of force—for good or evil—in the world. People who received power through dreams or waking visions became condensors through which power was channeled into the lives of other men and women.

You could seek for power, in the form of a guardian spirit, or a spirit could bestow power on you unsought. In the latter case you dared not refuse the gift; to do so would cost the life of one of your nearest and dearest relatives. Power could come from the world of nature, or it could be diffused from a material object such as a feather or a stone knife. Power could never be denied or disobeyed; most of the unhappiness of the world of men and women came either from conflicts of opposed powers or from the refusal of individuals to

116

accept or obey power which centered on them. It must have been healthy humility on my part not to claim to be the vehicle of a power.

The second time I spoke of my recurrent tipi dream, Elizabeth laughed a little. "It comes back to you the way they say power dreams used to return to people," she observed. "If you dream it clearly four times, we'll have to go to my old uncle and have him explain it to you."

"I've already dreamed it four times, I just haven't spoken about it," I said, and then went on to ask if women ever had power dreams in the old days. I was still alert for leads to the evasive religious information I had set out to get.

"Wait a minute, I'll ask Grandmother," Elizabeth replied, and she relayed the query. Grandmother answered that power dreams had been known to come to women, but that women usually dreamed about their homes and families. When the reason for the question was stated to her, she said positively that I had no need of a "guardian of the old gods" to explain my dream to me; I was dreaming about tipis because we were all thinking and talking about them and that was all there was to it. Elizabeth and I accepted the explanation willingly, especially since it coincided with our own college training in psychology.

Days went by. A weekend intervened. I went home for three days to do some more library research. Elizabeth and Grandmother planned to attend a Protestant church camp meeting while I was away. It seemed a source of innocent merriment for them and of complete boredom for me; so I willingly permitted our paths to diverge. If they had planned to attend some tribal ceremony, I would certainly have felt differently. I went home, and in my own bed there I dreamed of a succession of tipis.

When I reached Elizabeth's home Monday noon, I found

117

her waiting for me, with a puzzled expression on her face. "I saw my uncle this weekend," she greeted me.

"Did you?" I asked. "Which one?" Elizabeth had innumerable actual and titulary uncles—now mine, too—but I had not yet learned to distinguish them to my own satisfaction.

"The old one," said Elizabeth with a touch of impatience. "The one who is a guardian of a grandmother god."

"Well?" I inquired.

"He says for you to come and see him. He has things to tell you about the old days," Elizabeth announced flatly.

It had happened before. I had been sent for to come and listen to the talk of other elderly Indians, who were either too senile to think consecutively, or who wanted to impress me with the early introduction and immediate acceptance of Christianity in their tribe. I hesitated before I answered.

"He says he had a dream about you," Elizabeth reported impersonally. "He's blind. He says his eyes opened and he saw you. His power spirit was standing on one side of you and the grandmother god he guards was on the other. He says they ordered him to talk to you and tell you all he knows about religion."

I sat down abruptly on the bench in the arbor where we were talking, and stared at Elizabeth. This was unmistakeably an account of a power dream, precisely as they were recorded in ethnological literature, and it was my first encounter with a genuine one at first hand. I could hardly believe my ears.

"Of course," Elizabeth continued, "he's an old heathen, and my father says he was a regular rip in his younger days. But he's quieted down a lot now, and anyway he just uses his power for healing the other old people. They come to see him about their rheumatism and stomach upsets, and he

118

prays over them and waves incense in front of his god, and they go away feeling better for a while. That's all anybody could do for most of them, and it makes them happier, so it doesn't do anybody any harm. It may be rather a good thing."

"Elizabeth," I almost whispered, "will he talk to us? Honestly?"

"He's got to," Elizabeth informed me matter-of-factly. "If his power says to, he's got to do it."

"What about Grandmother?" I asked.

"Oh, she'll help my stepmother can watermelon pickles. They'll be busy for the next two weeks at least. You don't have to worry about her."

My hands were shaking with excitement. I clenched them into fists to still them. "Elizabeth—can you—is it all right —do you mind interpreting?"

"I've got to interpret," Elizabeth replied. "The power says I'm going to do it—and besides, I wouldn't miss it for anything. Here it is—just what we've been looking for all summer. Do you think I'm going to be left out now?"

I drew a deep breath, all doubts stilled, all problems solved. I turned to the car. "Well," I said impatiently, opening the door, "Come on. What are we waiting for?"

"It's quite a trip over there," Elizabeth agreed. "We'd better get started."

The car shuddered forward. On the drive, Elizabeth suddenly began to talk, and to talk about what she had been told of the old days. I had long suspected that she knew more about certain matters than she had ever admitted to me. Now, intent on briefing me for the encounter with her uncle, she relaxed her reserve, and for the first time she talked freely.

Now for the first time she assured me that the old religion of the tribe was still a going concern. Ten medicine bundles,

119

which Elizabeth referred to as "the ten grandmother gods," were still in the hands of ten traditional guardians. I asked what the bundles contained.

"I don't know," Elizabeth replied. "The last man who had the right to open them died fifty years ago. He had to do his ceremony in a dark tipi, by touch, so he couldn't see the gods, and he could never tell anybody what it was he felt. After he died nobody had the right to open the bundles, because he left no sons or nephews to carry on the ceremony."

"And even the guardians couldn't open them?"

"Not even the guardians."

"What are the grandmothers good for?" I inquired. Medicine bundles have many, and widely varying, powers. Sometimes they are curative in effect when invoked; sometimes they bring their owners or suppliants prowess in war; sometimes their guardians are able to forecast the future or to dispense love potions; sometimes their magic is black enough to kill if so commanded.

"Well," Elizabeth answered me, considering, "I suppose you could say that the grandmothers work rather like vacuum cleaners. They suck up all the evil that might come to the tribe, and hold it. As long as the bundles are safe, the whole tribe is safe, and no harm can come to anyone who belongs to it."

I was startled by the definite character of Elizabeth's reply. Anyone listening to us in ignorance of her personal background would have supposed that she accepted as the literal truth her statement of the character and abilities of the grandmother gods. In fact, that very impression came over me in spite of my previous knowledge. I refrained from asking her any questions on the point. Elizabeth might be going along with me to get the answers to the questions that had plagued me all summer; on the other hand, she might not. She seemed to know considerably more about the matter than I would have thought possible the day before.

We drove over a rise of ground, and saw before us an establishment of some size. In addition to the usual frame farm house and barns, there was an enormous vaulted brush arbor, a spread of chicken runs, and two tipis, each surrounded by a picket fence by way of a windbreak. Straight as a die between the two canvas cones, paralleling a gravel drive and connecting the house with the main line on the highway, there was a telephone wire.

"It's my sister Kate's place," Elizabeth explained. "Our old uncle lives with her, and so does her father-in-law. That one's a regular old hard-shelled pagan—he keeps one of the grandmothers, too, and he's a real old-timer about it. He won't ride in a car, because he says none of those men (they're like priests), should never have anything to do with machinery. Some of the others ride in cars, but he takes a wagon and team when he doesn't feel like riding horseback. He won't use a telephone, but whenever he wants to talk to somebody, he makes my brother-in-law call the person and talk for him. He never speaks to me, because he says I've turned my back on my people's gods and gone over to the white man's ways. I have, too," she added conscientiously.

I turned the car into the driveway that ran beneath the telephone wire. At a point about fifty feet from the house there was a turn around, with a minor drive leading from it to each tipi. Without thinking, I started to take the path to the left.

"No," said Elizabeth, abruptly for her, "you go the other way. That tipi you're headed for belongs to the other old man, not to my uncle. We don't want to bother *him*."

I twisted the wheel, and headed out of the turn around on the right-hand road. As I drew up before the smaller of

121

the two tipis, the gate in its picket fence opened, and an old man stepped through it. He stood waiting for us, facing the car.

He was tiny and bent now and twisted with age and arthritis. His hands and feet were like a child's—a doll's—the delicate, cared-for hands and feet of a man who has never done manual labor of any sort, or walked more than the few yards from his dwelling to his waiting saddle horse. A priest and an aristocratic priest—he fitted well into the old pattern.

His head was disproportionately large and its bony structure was surprisingly heavy in contrast to the light body. The sparse white braids that hung beside his red-painted cheeks and tangled his dangling silver earrings were wrapped in turquoise-blue wool yarn. His blue denim work shirt was immaculate and freshly laundered. So were his too-large khaki work pants. On his feet were moccasins entirely covered with beadwork of blue and white.

The eyes in the great head were blank, but the face that turned towards us was not expressionless; it was split with a wide and welcoming grin. And the voice in which the old man spoke to Elizabeth was still a good masculine voice, deep and sound.

"He says he can see you," Elizabeth reported to me. "His eyes are closed, but he can see you plainly." She waited a moment while the old man spoke again, then resumed her translation. "I guess he can, at that," she observed. "He says you've got on a blue-and-white striped dress made out of crinkly material like a bedspread—I told you, you ought to iron that seersucker, and not just hang it up to dry—and you've got hair like a bay mare's mane, and your eyes are light-colored. He says people who have power dreams often have eyes like that. And he says your car belongs here, but it's branded differently from other cars—he talks as if he could see that university license plate."

I started to reply, but before I could form my words the old man spoke again.

"He says for us to come in the tipi," Elizabeth relayed to me.

Obediently I followed them. The old man felt his way with a stick he held in one hand; the fingers of the other ran lightly over a cord that had been stretched from the gate in the fence to the doorway of the tipi.

We stooped to enter the low door in the canvas wall. When I again stood upright, I saw that Elizabeth was seated on the left, the woman's side of the tipi. The old man sat facing the entrance, in the place of honor and authority. Above his head hung a diamond-shaped case of rawhide, with painted symbols dimly visible on its time-darkened surface. That, I realized with a jerk of excitement, must be the medicine bundle that held the grandmother god.

Our host gestured me to a place between Elizabeth and himself, and I sat down on the ground, folding my legs correctly beneath me to the left, and waited. Conversational preliminaries followed: the weather, the sad state of the crops, Elizabeth's mare and its newly dropped foal, my usual place of residence and existing family.

Question and answer followed one another, between informant and interviewer. I was thoroughly familiar with the process by now, and responded almost mechanically when my turn came, sitting there with my notebook and pencil in my lap. The old man must grow thoroughly accustomed to them. He might be officially blind, but he was also disconcertingly discerning. He seemed able to do a good accu-

123

rate piece of verbal description when the notion struck him. He might be able to see more, actually, than those around him thought he could.

"He says," Elizabeth began when casual matters had been disposed of, "that he has been waiting for you all day. He has much to tell you, and he is eager to begin. His grandmother god and his own power have told him to speak, and to speak to you. Once each guardian had a woman to help him; a young woman, of his own family. Now you are a member of our family, and he is getting old. The time has come for him to tell you what you are supposed to know."

I opened the fresh, clean notebook, and wrote the date with a new pencil, at the top of the first page. "Tell him to begin," I instructed Elizabeth.

The old man smiled again, and spoke, and held out his hand.

"He says for you to give him cigarettes," Elizabeth translated.

I took a fresh pack from my purse, and passed it over. He opened it by touch, extracted a cigarette, shifted his weight so he could take a match from his hip pocket, and, when the cigarette was drawing well, flipped the spent match accurately into the firehole in the center of the tipi floor. Pencil poised, I waited while the cigarette was consumed, the smoker meanwhile wrapped in a visible blue haze, as in thought.

"He says," Elizabeth began when her uncle at last spoke again, "that these things are serious. They are sacred. They must be spoken of carefully. First there is a story you must hear. It takes all day to tell and it can only be interrupted once—at noon, for dinner. If you can come early tomorrow morning, he will start with that story and then go on to the other things you are supposed to know on other days."

"Let everything be done decently and in order," I quoted from the prayer book on which I was raised. "All right. Tell him we will come back early in the morning. And be sure you tell him that we will pay him fifty cents an hour for all the time we spend talking."

"He says he will be as rich as an Osage with oil wells on his land," Elizabeth laughed when these words had been repeated and answered. We rose and made our adieus. As we talked again of unimportant matters and the strain of our attention on each other relaxed, we heard the repeated tingling of the telephone bell from inside the house.

Outside the tipi, when we emerged, another old man stood. He looked at us without speaking, and turned, and strode away in the direction of the other picket-ringed canvas shelter. "My brother-in-law's father," Elizabeth said. "I bet he was listening to everything we said in there."

My dreams that night, when I slept at all, were concerned with a riot of tipis. They swarmed around me, they danced, I could hear a drum beating time to their antics. If that wasn't a power dream, I reflected when the banging of the alarm clock interrupted their activities, I hope I never have one.

Our welcome, when we entered the old man's tipi, was cordial. I reopened my notebook, and wrote a second date on the line directly beneath the first.

"Tell him I'm ready," I directed Elizabeth. The old man began to talk.

Conflicting expressions chased one another across Elizabeth's face. "Something's funny," she muttered to me, aside. "This isn't a religious story—it's the kind they tell to children. This is a story about the Tricky One and how the deer lost their teeth. Well, maybe it will work into the other one."

125

I sat and waited for a break in the story and the beginning of the translation. My eyes wandered about the tipi, and rested from time to time on the painted case above the old man's head. Over the slow sounds of the Indian voices beside me, I heard the telephone bell again. The religion must indeed be active, I thought idly, remembering the dozens of tire tracks printed on the dust of the turn around that morning. I had noticed them especially because, when we drove away the night before, only the tracks of the university car had been visible on the windswept ground. A mob of people must have come to the place after we went home. And they must have come because of the grandmother god, for there were no signs in the yard outside the house that a dance or other social celebration had taken place there. I turned my attention back to Elizabeth as she began to interpret.

The story about the Tricky One came to its usual abrupt, O. Henry-esque ending. Elizabeth and I sat, and looked blankly at one another.

"Maybe it's a warm-up," I suggested, dutifully writing down what Elizabeth had just dictated.

"I don't believe so," she replied. "I think something must have gone wrong."

The old man began another nursery tale, and I recorded it in its turn. There was no question about the matter this time. He was avoiding giving us the information he had promised. My heart sank. I had been hooked again. Another old man with nothing much to say, who wanted to be paid for saying it. This one time, at least, I had expected something different.

The third story was unfamiliar, and I began to feel more hopeful, but the fourth was again a standard thing, one that was included in all the anthologies of Plains Indian litera-

126

ture that I had ever read. I put it down for what it was worth as a variant, but at its end I faced the situation squarely. He was not giving me any information.

"Tell him," I directed Elizabeth, "that these are good stories, but anybody can tell them. Tell him we have come to him to learn the things that nobody else can teach us. Tell him we are waiting for him to start the long story that he promised to tell us."

There was a lengthy pause when Elizabeth had finished speaking. The old uncle took the battered cigarette package that remained from the day before out of his shirt pocket, and extracted from an inner corner the last cigarette. He tilted his buttocks, removed a match from his hip pocket, and smoked moodily. He looked tired and depressed. At last, when the cigarette butt smoldered on a heap of its predecessors in the fire-pit, he spoke.

"He says he cannot tell you," Elizabeth reported expressionlessly.

"Does he want another interpreter? One who is not a Christian?"

This problem had not arisen before in our encounters with the older people, but I felt that we might have to deal with it.

"He says no. He wants me to interpret whatever he tells you."

"Does he want us to go through some kind of ceremony first?"

I was prepared for anything. I hoped that Elizabeth was, too.

"He says no. No ceremony is necessary."

"Then what *is* the matter?"

Again, there was a long pause. Encouragingly, I produced another package of cigarettes, and passed it over.

"He says he cannot tell us," Elizabeth repeated. We seemed to have reached a dead end.

"Let's go in the house and talk to your sister," I suggested. "She may know what the matter is." Perhaps, I thought, if the old man had a chance to think things over some more, he might feel differently about talking—feel as he had the day before.

"All right," Elizabeth assented, listlessly.

She explained to her uncle that we would return, and we left the old man drearily smoking in the back of the tipi, under the bundle that contained his god.

Kate, Elizabeth's much older sister, a woman upholstered as comfortably as an easy chair, was padding around the kitchen, preparing lunch. When we explained the situation, she wiped her hands on her apron, and smiled a little sadly.

"I sure feel bad about what happen," she assured us, "but you know how those old-timers are. When they don' wan' somethin' done, they don'."

"But he *did* want to tell us!" I wailed.

"Sure he did. I know that. He talk about it all summer; seem like he di'n't have nothin' else on his min'. He sure wan' to tell you ever'thin' he know."

"That's what I thought!"

"An' he still wan' work with you. He still wan' you to come an' write down old-timer stories. He know lots of them —good ones—stories nobody else know. He wan' you to write them down."

"That's fine; I'll be glad to. He's a good storyteller. But why won't he tell us the things he said he was going to?"

The sister hesitated, obviously embarrassed. Her hands twisted her apron into a wad of calico. "Well," she said, after some thought, "did you see the car tracks outside?"

128

"Yes," we answered together.

"Well. Yesterday evenin', after you lef', all them other guardians was here. An' they all tole him the same thin'. If he tole you what he was aimin' to, they'd put a curse on him so's he'd die. So he's scare'."

"But he had a power dream. *I* had power dreams!"

"I know it. He tole me all about his dreams—and yours, too. An' he's scare' his power's goin' to kill him if those other guardians don't. But he's worse scare' of them. He don't know what to do, and he don't know what you can do."

Elizabeth and I consulted one another with our eyes. This was too big for us to protest against. Like a pair of solemn lizards on a fence, we nodded at each other. Behind us, on the shelf of the kitchen cabinet, the telephone jingled noisily.

"All right," I said, finally. "We'll stay here and work, and we'll write down the other old-timer stories if he wants to tell them."

"You won't say nothin' to him 'bout how I tole you?" the sister asked.

"We won't say anything," I assured her regretfully, as I rose and prepared to return to the tipi. At the kitchen door I paused, and turned around. It had occurred to me that I might still be on the threshhold of the supernatural; that telepathetic communication might have been used to defeat me. "How did the other guardians find out what was going on?" I asked.

"Oh," said the sister, turning back to her cooking, "my husban's father made him call ever'body up on the telephone, and tell 'em to get on over here for a council."

CHAPTER 10

THE SONG OF BEOWULF

E LIZABETH, her old uncle and I worked together on mythology for another week. My summer's research funds were exhausted, and I left the Kiowa country to return to the university. At the end of the winter of graduate work, I was surprised and delighted to be notified that I had again been awarded funds for independent research, to complete the work I had already begun.

Mythology was the topic that had been cut short the year before. I wrote to Elizabeth immediately, to ask whether she would have a vacation from her government job, whether she would be willing to spend all or part of it interpreting for me, and whether she thought her old uncle could and would continue as our informant. She answered "Yes" to all my questions, almost by return mail. I lost no time in packing my clothes and loading the car for departure to the country south of Anadarko. I spent a few days visiting with the Camp family and renewing the previous summer's friendships. Then Elizabeth arrived, and we got down to business.

There were three of us under the shade of the brush arbor: the old uncle, and Elizabeth, and me. We sat, enclosed and protected, lapped in shadow that held back the blue haze of the heat of midsummer. Beyond our shelter, the gray brown of heat-seared grass quivered and flickered across the flat and down the bank to the brittle trees rimming the gully. Through that gully, when autumn brought the rains again, red, muddy water would crawl. This was western Oklahoma, during a year of drought.

Under the arch of the arbor there was no Oklahoma, and the years were so far away as to be unnumbered. The old man sat on a child's stool, for time had shrunk him to a child's size. He was bent forward, his lean shoulders pressed against the faded blue of his cotton shirt. His skinny braids, wrapped in clean green yarns, swung beside his cheeks, and the tips of the plaits just brushed the bones of his shoulders. From time to time he sucked on a home-made brown paper cigarette, and each time, after he had expelled a thin trail of gray-blue smoke, he spat deliberately and precisely into a tin can that stood before him on the ground. Occasionally, he moved a finger to push the copper bracelet further up his right wrist, away from the rheumatic joint it was supposed to ease.

Elizabeth sat on a cushion on the ground, with her legs folded to one side beneath her. On her face was the pained, disapproving expression of a mother who hears her children discussing a slightly obscene motion picture. After all, Elizabeth was an ardent Christian, and we, two people whom ordinarily she liked and admired, had spent whole days telling and retelling the old, pagan legends of the tribe to which she and the old man belonged.

Now it lacked an hour until noon. The old man was getting slightly bored, and, consequently, restless. Elizabeth shook her head at him when he stirred and spoke. Then she turned to me anxiously.

"He says these stories are for children. He says you are a grown woman and have been to college. If you had children of your own, he could understand why you would like to learn these tales. But you aren't married, even. Why do you spend so much time writing our old stories down? Haven't the white people any stories of their own? He wants you to answer, not me; he isn't satisfied with what I tell him."

Because I, too, was bored—after all, some of the stories were extremely childish, mere plays on the words of a language I did not know—I said, idly, "Of course white people have stories. Lots of stories, some of them maybe older than these. I want to write down his stories so I can study them and compare them with the ones I know from my own people. Perhaps his tribe and mine knew each other, farther back than anyone now can count."

Was this not a satisfactory explanation of the ethnological collection of folklore, for the study of world-wide distributions? I had a sneaking suspicion that the professor back at the university would be proud of me. I had over-simplified, perhaps, but my explanation was certainly comprehensible. Elizabeth nodded approvingly, and so did the old man, when she had translated what I said.

It was immediately clear that besides understanding, he was pleased with the idea. He raised his head as he listened, and his blind eyes looked toward me. One of his rare smiles cracked his brown face into a maze of wrinkles, deep and shallow. He lifted his hand to hush Elizabeth, and he spoke decisively. Elizabeth turned back to me, rather helplessly.

"He says it is a good idea. He thinks it is sensible. White

people are smarter than he thought. That white man who comes to ask him about history, he never explains. The old man says you are better than the man. You tell him why you do these things, and you never ask him questions his god won't let him answer."

The old man had spoken to us of the white man and his questions about history before. I had come into the field the summer before knowing that the Kiowa tribe had not been studied for fifty years, and supposing that I was the only person interested in studying it now. But it had not been long after the beginning of the second season before rumors reached me that there was "a man talking to the old people about history." Elizabeth's uncle had been so anxious to work with me that it had never crossed my mind that someone else might have since begun to interview him.

But so it was. The man was a graduate student of ethnology; that was as evident as the fact that he must have come from somewhere out of the state. By piecing together the fragments that had come to me from our mutual informant, I had gathered that my rival—for so I had come to think of him—was taking a direct, robust, man-to-man approach. Naturally, he used his own interpreter, a young man he had picked up in Agency Town, and with whom he had been seen drinking beer in the evenings. That was regarded as unethical, as well as illegal, in the school where I had been trained.

Also, I had gathered that my competitor was trying to elicit information about religion by asking leading questions and disguising his approach as an interest in history. That was—if possible—slightly worse than unethical in my book. In fact, if I had been pressed to define such conduct, I doubt if I could have found a single word sufficiently condemnatory.

Consequently, I avoided meeting the young man from the other university, afraid that I would lose my temper and express my opinion of him should we ever come face to face. It had been by accident that I had discovered that he had worked with *my* old man earlier in the summer, and that he had said that he would return again later.

My rival had not come on the scene until my second summer in the field with Elizabeth's tribe. He had stolen my informant before I could leave the university for that summer, then had returned the old man to me temporarily while he worked with someone else, and would reclaim Elizabeth's uncle as soon as I again left the field. Only the fact that we had already established a close relationship made it possible for the three of us to work together after such an interruption. Now, it seemed, I had unexpectedly found and used a means of strengthening our *rapport*, and, it could be, of securing further information.

So I smiled at the old uncle, although he could not see me, and agreed with his agreement with my initial statement. Then, the burden of boredom lifted momentarily from my shoulders, I once again poised my pencil above my notebook. "Please, Elizabeth, tell him I am ready to go on. Does he know another story about the Tricky One?"

Elizabeth repeated the request, and the old man shook his head. Startled, she spoke again. His face, his shoulders, his whole body, suddenly expressed mulish contradiction. He spoke incisively. Elizabeth turned to me.

"He says again he thinks comparing stories is a good idea. He says for you to tell him one of yours, so he will know what they are like. He says he is an old man and he is going to die—some day, I suppose—and he would like to hear one of the old, old stories of the white people before he goes."

134

There seemed to be no alternative. If I refused, the old man could turn his back on me and give all the precious information encased in his frail skull to my rival. This reversal of the roles of informant and ethnographer was vaguely disturbing, yet, at the same time, it was funny, too. I winked at Elizabeth. "Tell him to wait a minute while I think. I've been concentrating on his stories too much. Let me remember—"

"Tell him a Bible story," suggested Elizabeth, ever alert for converts.

I paused. Some of the more rousing yarns in the Old Testament—Joshua, Samson, or Judith, for instance—had their possibilities. But somehow that seemed like cheating; cheating Elizabeth as well as the old man. Then, suddenly, an idea came to me. "Tell him," I said, "that this is the story about The Brave Warrior and the Water Monster."

Elizabeth relayed the information. The old man nodded and smiled, pleased as a child, and rolled himself another cigarette. He settled comfortably on his child's stool, and prepared to listen. As boldly as I could, I began to tell the story of Beowulf.

"There was once a great chief," I commenced, "who built himself a big white tipi on the top of a hill. And he gathered all the young men in his tribe around him—all the best fighting young men, that is, and formed them into a Warrior Society.

"Down at the foot of the hill there was a river, and a great pool. The water was so deep and still that it was black. At the bottom of the black lake, in a tipi she had built of black stone, there lived the old Witch of the Water, with her son—"

Very few changes were needed in the telling. Shields,

spears, bows and arrows, were the weapons as much of these Indians as of the ancient Angles. And Grendel, the water monster, and the old Witch, his mother, were well within the aboriginal pattern of legendary behavior. Even today I flatter myself that I made of the under-water fight a stirring thing. Elizabeth was entranced, and her eyes were shining with excitement as she translated the story. The old man followed it with charmed interest.

"Tell it again," he demanded, when it was over, and I obligingly repeated the tale. This time he followed the telling even more closely, repeating Elizabeth's words, and paralleling the thoughts of the story with the gestures of sign language.

When Grendel's mother was slain for the second time, the sun stood directly above the roof of the arbor. Elizabeth stood up. "Lunch time," she announced prosaically, and we helped the old man to his feet. Together the three of us went slowly across from the small, old person's arbor to the big one that was the family's living room in summer.

Here we found that, as usual, the space was crowded, not only with the members of Elizabeth's sister's family, but with visitors. Today there was an unusually large number of the latter, many of them the old man's contemporaries of the buffalo-hunting days.

"They've been to the agency for their rental checks," Elizabeth informed me. "They always stop off here for a visit and a meal on the way home."

The old people and the men of the family ate first, according to long-established custom. We younger women: Elizabeth and her sister, the female visitors of their age, and myself, waited until the others had finished. While we waited, and some of the women served, we watched and listened. It was understood by all the family that Elizabeth and I could stand and look on, and even eavesdrop, when we wanted to. Riches of information often came to us that way.

Our old man bowed his head above his plate, and uttered a lengthy grace, addressed to the Powers Unseen. There was a chorus of approving ejaculations when he finished, and then the food was consumed in silence. Eating was always a two-fold process to these old people; a serious occupation in itself, and at the same time an interruption of other business. No one delayed a meal by talking. When it was over, and the table was as bare as if the diners had been locusts, the old people shifted and their mood changed with their places. Men and women alike settled on the benches that edged the arbor, and we younger women cleared and reset the table, and took our places for our own meal. Elizabeth "asked the Blessing," this time in English and in a stereotyped formula. We ate as silently and seriously as the older people had, for by now they had begun to talk, and we were listening.

I heard my own name, the Story-Writing Woman, mentioned several times, questioningly. The old man answered, as nearly as I could tell, enthusiastically. Then there was an intense, a definite question. In the silence that followed it, I heard his voice begin. "Once upon a time—" I was by now thoroughly familiar with the Indian words that marked the opening of a story. I turned my head, and out of the corner of my eye I watched his gestures. Arms above his head, at full stretch—a big tipi. The sign for man, and then the sign for a leader. Many young men around him, all armed warriors. Suddenly, I perceived what was happening. My informant was telling the story of Beowulf.

Elizabeth was shaking on the bench beside me, quivering

137

with smothered, choking mirth. Under her breath, she began to interpret. And at whatever cost to my vanity, I must admit that the old man made a better story of it than I had. A born, a creative storyteller, he added bits here and there to round out the tale and make it richer. So must Beowulf have gone from mouth to ear, and on, improved, to the next hearer, in all the centuries before the saga was written down.

The audience loved it. They interrupted the speaker, from time to time, with approving "Hoh!"s. They followed and imitated his gestures. Their heads nodded; some of them even forgot to smoke. Here was a new story, and one that was perfectly comprehensible to them. They were completely outside themselves in their enjoyment.

The company stayed on after the story ended, discussing it, discussing stories of their own, finally, endlessly, gossiping. It was useless to try to work through the afternoon with such competition at hand to draw our informant's thoughts away. I helped Elizabeth and the other women wash the dishes, and finally drove away through the afternoon heat to my boardinghouse.

I went back to work the next morning, and the storytelling resumed in a pleasant, friendly, and refreshed atmosphere. And so, with complete *rapport*, it continued for the following weeks, until the time came for me to go back to the university. Tearfully, for farewells to those in old age can be dreadfully certain, we all said good-by. At the last, Elizabeth left the old man, and ran to the car.

"He says to tell you that man is coming back here next week," she said. "He wants you to know that he will not tell him any of the stories he has told to you. He will not tell anything you would not want him to tell."

138

It was almost exactly two years later that I opened the current issue of *Anthropological America* to an article entitled: "Occurrence of a Beowulf-like Myth Among North American Indians." It was signed by a graduate of an important university, appended to whose name were the initials and date signifying a shiny-new Ph.D.

CHAPTER 11

FATHER-IN-LAW TABU

THE Indian tribe with which I did my first real field research was still completing the difficult transition from the Stone Age to the Age of Mechanization. Even sixty years earlier, the western range country where these people lived had been unfenced; livestock had been unknown, and buffalo had abounded in the area. White men had been present only as small clusters of border troops who made forays from their stockaded forts when absolute necessity demanded reprisals on the Indians for damage done to the few white settlers who attempted to penetrate the region.

Consequently, for a few brief years I was privileged to know intimately men and women who could clearly remember when flint-and-pyrites were replaced by matches as a means of making a fire. They could remember when their people lived almost entirely on meat, varied slightly and occasionally with handfuls of small wild fruits. They had seen their rivers run clear, and they had seen plows break

140

the plains and the lifeblood of the land turn the streams crimson. Most vividly, they could remember the social customs of the old days, and when they could they observed them.

One institution which the old people preserved to some degree was polygamy. In their youth they had known plural marriage as an economic necessity. War and hunting took the lives of young men, and surplus women had to be cared for in some way. A man often married the woman of his choice, then, as they matured, her younger sisters. Should he be killed, his brother or one of his cousins—whoever was in a position to afford the luxury—inherited the entire collection of wives. Plural wives were not necessarily related. Sisterhood was generally regarded as desirable, however, since it was a guarantee of peace at the family fireside.

Kate, the older sister of my friend and interpreter, Elizabeth, had married into a family where polygamy was still a going concern. At the time that the government Indian service required most men to give up their plural wives, Kate's father-in-law, like a few of the other older men, had been allowed to keep his. He was a medicine man—a *shaman,* to use the technical word—and his wives were his assistants when he treated his patients. For that reason, and because all the people in what seemed a peaceful menage were elderly, the government made an exception in the case of Old Man Sitting-Standing.

I was made keenly aware of the old man on a Monday morning. Elizabeth and I were interviewing her old uncle, who made his home with Kate's family. We all sat in the brush arbor that was the family's summer living quarters, chatting composedly. Suddenly, Elizabeth arose and turned her back on the entrance to the arbor. Our flow of conversation continued unabated, but her abrupt reversal of position startled me, and for a moment I lost the train of thought.

"What happened?" I asked. Elizabeth's present situation on a backless bench facing a blank wall seemed to me needlessly uncomfortable.

"Kate's father-in-law," she responded. "That makes him mine, too, and he's a real old-timer, remember? He doesn't like me to talk to him or go near him or touch him or even look at him." She sighed reminiscently. "Last winter he ate something that didn't agree with him—bad canned meat his second wife had put up, likely. Both his wives were away visiting, and Kate had to take care of him. They both nearly lost their minds—he was so modest about having her around."

I had heard of this father-in-law tabu, and had surmised that it operated in the tribe. "How did they get around it?" I inquired.

"Oh," said Elizabeth, matter-of-factly, "they did what everyone else does—when they wanted to say something to each other, they talked to a beam in the ceiling. It was like using a telephone, rather. She'd say, 'Please tell this honored old man to take his medicine,' and he'd say, 'Please tell that respectable young woman I don't want to,'—all sorts of things like that. They managed, but she never did get to give him a bath, even when the government doctor said he had to have one. He made Kate send Henry, her husband, thirty miles to get his mother and bring her home so she could bathe the old man. It was dead of winter, and cold, but Henry's mother had to come back with Henry in the pick-up, whether she wanted to or not, to give her husband a bath. Those old-timers are particular."

A brisk tapping of fingers on the bench where he sat warned us that our own old-timer, our joint uncle, was ready to get on with the business of the day. This was a discussion of the way feathers were put on arrows in the old hunting days.

That second summer I was in the field Elizabeth and I shared Kate's spare bedroom. By that time my adoption into the family was an accepted fact to everyone. I was a sister of Elizabeth and Kate, and my duties, responsibilities, and privileges were no less than Elizabeth's own.

So I found myself, by extension of the custom that made me a potential wife of Kate's husband, standing in her relationship to her father-in-law. I could not say "Good morning" to Sitting-Standing if I came into a room where he had established himself. My back must be turned; if that were impossible, my eyes must be averted. I must be careful about long sleeves and high necks and pulled-down skirts in his presence, in spite of the midsummer heat. And the old man was equally careful. If he could, he left a room as soon as I entered; otherwise, he turned his back and ignored me with the most profound politeness and respect.

This was annoying because I wanted him as an informant. To have such a source of information on healing customs within reach and still inaccessible was maddening. No amount of other information quite compensated for that loss. But to talk to Sitting-Standing was out of the question. He was my father-in-law, and the more remote our relations from now on, the more cordial.

Monday morning, I soon learned, was an important time in the life of my extended family. On Monday morning Sitting-Standing changed wives. Henry's mother, the senior wife, lived with her son and Kate. Wife Number Two lived in a house of her own about a quarter-mile away. Between the two properties ran a creek, and Sitting-Standing owned the water-rights and the land adjacent. The creek bed furnished a handy dividing-line. Neither wife was supposed to cross it.

Wife Number Two, I discovered by degrees, had the reputation of being a tartar. Her name was Judith; apparently it had been bestowed by some missionary with a profound knowledge of the Bible and its personalities, and a sense of humor. She was not a sister of Henry's mother, but an outsider. Judith had been away to school, and spoke some English. Henry's aunt, his father's previous second wife, had died some time before. Judith was a much younger woman, and the family feeling was that Father had married her in a rash moment, simply to keep up his two-wife franchise.

On Monday morning, then, there was always a bustle in the household, and Elizabeth and I were always delayed in getting down to work. Sitting-Standing had to pack. He gathered together his clean shirts, and deposited his soiled linen in a lordly heap in the middle of the kitchen floor. Kate owned a washing-machine and a gasoline iron. Her mother-in-law was supposed to do the laundry. I often wondered whether Sitting-Standing really knew that his wife thought that the pump handle of the hand washer was attached to a supernatural spirit, and that the fire in the gasoline iron was of diabolic origin. Naturally, she firmly refused to touch either object, and Kate or Elizabeth did the old man's laundry.

While the shirts were being sorted, Henry was dispatched to the pasture to rope his father's saddle horse. This might involve a stroll of two or three miles, but Sitting-Standing was adamant. No horse of his should be confined in a corral overnight. His son was young and strong; let him go forth and herd his father's riding horse in the traditional way. Poor Henry always returned leading the horse, which he was forbidden to ride, hours behind hand with his farm work for the day, but invariably polite to his father, who supervised the saddling of the horse with minute attention to detail.

At precisely nine o'clock in the morning, everything was ready. Clean clothes wrapped in a newspaper parcel, braids swathed in blue or green yarns, a Stetson or a broad-brimmed straw hat on his head, Sitting-Standing approached his horse on the right side and hauled himself up into the enormous rocking-chair stock saddle. He refused to mount any horse white-man's fashion, from the left.

Sitting-Standing adjusted his ponderous rump in the saddle. He checked on the string that tied the parcel of clean shirts to the pommel. He gathered up the reins, and he waited. Henry's mother, her hair loosened, her back bent, her whole attitude one of complete, reverent awe, emerged from the kitchen door. Before her she carried a rawhide bundle which held the old man's medicines. Tied to it, and dangling from it, was a red-painted rawhide rattle made from a buffalo scrotum.

Henry's mother stretched her arms above her head—she was a small woman—and her husband condescendingly relieved her of her obviously weighty burden. He tied it to his saddle horn, shook the reins, and clucked to the horse. They moved deliberately forward. Then on the opposite side of the creek, two hundred yards away, we could plainly see Sitting-Standing draw rein and the horse stop. Judith emerged from her house, and the ceremony of dismounting, a reversal of the previous one, took place.

On the following Monday morning at the same time, the proceeding would again be reversed, with one difference. Judith was expected to catch the horse herself, besides providing clean linens and breakfast. Henry, who was a good-natured soul, often volunteered to relieve his stepmother of this job, but she always refused his help. It was her privilege, she declared, to do everything possible to help her husband in his great task in life—healing the sick.

As time went on, it was more and more apparent that Judith was sand in the cream of an otherwise pleasant family life. Sometimes Sitting-Standing's return to Henry's mother was delayed until ten or eleven o'clock on Monday morning, to the old man's evident annoyance. Once at least Judith insisted that the shirts he brought with him were not properly washed, and did the whole bundle of laundry over. This was not too successful an effort, for Judith was a casual housekeeper, and her ironing showed it. On the following Monday Sitting-Standing brought a double quantity of laundry to Henry's house and commanded that it be done properly.

Sitting-Standing took great pleasure in his grandchildren, and whatever his relations with his first wife were, his one evident joy at Henry's house was playing with the little ones. Judith had no children and no grandchildren, but she took to sending pressing invitations to Kate to bring or send the children to her house—the old man missed them so when he was away from them. Sometimes Kate accepted the invitations and sent the children across the creek; at other times she refused. "If he misses them so much, let him come over and see them," she declared to Henry, who looked worried but kept out of what must have seemed to him entirely an affair for the women.

Often we heard shrieks from across the creek. Judith was berating her husband. What she said had fervor and point, if I were to judge from the laughter of Elizabeth and her uncle, as we sat under the arbor. Elizabeth refused to interpret. "I don't want you to know that Indians have such words," she said to cushion her denial.

Once we saw Judith fly from her kitchen door, her braids

straight out behind her like twin tails on a kite. After her a parcel of laundry hurtled through the air to strike the limb of a plum tree by the kitchen door and burst, scattering shirts in all directions. Hours later they still hung on the tree and the porch rail and littered the ground, until Judith meekly returned to gather them all together. She did not wash them herself, but brought them across to Kate. She told us then that she had attempted to refold the laundry and put it away in a drawer, and that her husband was annoyed because she had interfered with his affairs.

"Oh, he surely wouldn't get that mad over such a little thing," I said to Elizabeth when Judith had gone.

"He can if he wants to," she informed me. "A husband has the right to do anything he likes to his wife. He can beat her. He can even kill her if he takes a notion." Her black eyes grew round at the thought. "Maybe he will some day," she said thoughtfully.

"Kill her?"

"Well, beat her, anyhow."

Undoubtedly the uncertainty of Sitting-Standing's marital state added excitement to my field research. This was ethnology-on-the-hoof—the actual working out, before my own eyes, of almost legendary customs. I took to making notes on Judith's offenses, and spending a good part of each weekend, while I waited for next Monday morning's thrilling episode, taking bets with myself as to what it would include.

There was the Monday morning when Sitting-Standing, all ready to go, even to the medicine bundle tied to the saddle horn, sent Henry back into the house for his riding whip. We all anticipated the worst, especially when he held it in his hand as he followed Judith into the house, but there were no screams then or later from a chastised wife. Instead, it developed that Sitting-Standing had decided to train his horse himself for the quarter-horse races at the county fair.

But two weeks later it was apparent that something really dreadful had happened. Sitting-Standing returned to Henry's house on a Saturday morning. As he dismounted, he volunteered the only comment on Judith's behavior I ever heard him utter. "A man came to see her," he stated.

Titillated, Elizabeth and I peered around the corner of the arbor. The government farmer's car was parked before Judith's house. Later we learned that her corn field was one selected for experimental planting of a new type of seed corn.

But apparently her husband's reaction gave Judith ideas, and she began to play coy. More and more often the farmer's car was parked before the house. Judith sent him word to come and look at the sprouting corn; at the borers that attacked it; at her watermelon vines; at the plum tree, which was not bearing as well as usual. And the farmer, an earnest young man, not long escaped from agricultural college, dutifully came and looked and returned to the agency and, we supposed, wrote reports. He lived with his wife and small son in Agency Town, and his life, when not consumed by matters domestic, was absorbed by his work. He certainly never thought of Judith as anything but an adjunct to an experimental corn field.

Judith herself maintained the nose-lofty attitude of Caesar's wife. *Anyone* could see that the farmer came to her house on business, and only on business. Anyone, especially a husband, who thought otherwise, was mad. Of course, if the farmer *found* business on her place, she had to be polite to him. How could she do anything else? The Indians were supposed to cooperate with the government employees, weren't they?

Sitting-Standing regarded her with grim suspicion. On the

Monday mornings when he returned to his first wife's home, he drew audible sighs of relief as he dismounted. His was the attitude of a traveling man entering a first-class hotel after a long interval of poor ones. But he usually sat where he could see across the creek to Judith's house, and he watched the comings and goings there with a lowering face. Once he instructed Henry to ask me if I possessed a pair of see-far glasses, like those the Army officers at the near-by fort used to observe artillery fire.

On my next trip home, I brought back a pair of opera glasses. Sitting-Standing was delighted with them, as soon as he learned how to hold them, and spent hours leveling them at the farmer's car, and the demurely closed door of Judith's house.

How long matters might have gone on, I cannot guess. Judith was determined to wean her husband from his first wife and her family; the husband, a die-hard traditionalist, was determined not to be weaned, but to break Judith of what he decidedly considered to be bad habits.

By the end of the summer the riding whip was part of his costume. Mounted or afoot, he wore its strap around his wrist like a bracelet, and when he looked through the opera glasses at Judith's house the end of the whip lashed the dust like the tail of an angry cat. If he saw Judith, shaded by a huge black umbrella, emerge from the kitchen door and accompany the farmer to the high growth of the corn field, the sidewise movement became a series of vicious ups and downs, beating on the earth like a war drum.

The break came, as might have been predicted, on a hot Monday morning. Henry had brought the horse from the pasture, and held it, saddled and bridled, before the kitchen door. Kate had tied the bundle of laundry to the pommel, and joined me in the arbor, where we waited with Elizabeth,

149

out of the way of our joint father-in-law's appearance in the kitchen door. Henry's mother was waiting in the kitchen with the medicine bundle. Sitting-Standing appeared, and, before mounting, leveled his opera glasses at the house across the creek. The farmer's offending car was parked directly before the kitchen door, and a trail of smoke rose from the kitchen chimney. Even where we stood, the heavy summer air was additionally laden with the thick fragrance of fresh-made coffee. We had finished our breakfast and washed the dishes long before.

With a bellow like that of a wounded buffalo, Sitting-Standing leapt into his saddle. Even as a young man, he could not have done a neater or faster job of mounting. He hammered the horse with his heavy rawhide quirt, and the horse, fresh as the morning and trained to run, flattened itself over the dry grass and down the slope. We saw wings of water rise on either side of the rider as he tore through the creek, and the horse jerk back on its haunches when he drew rein before the kitchen door.

The door opened, and Judith and the farmer appeared. Judith lifted her starched cotton skirt as she started down the steps, affording all of us a glimpse of ravishing new beaded moccasins. The other hand clutched her open umbrella, as, oblivious of her enraged husband, she turned to make some killing remark to the farmer, who followed her.

The whip lash struck the umbrella and glanced off. Judith wasted no time looking to see what had caused the shock she had felt through the steel ferule. Abandoning all pretense of coyness, she ran down the slope, splashed through the creek, and, breathing heavily, gained the arbor where Elizabeth and I clung to each other in helpless, horrified mirth. Behind her, his horse belly-flat to the ground, his whip rising and falling in furious, indiscriminate blows, came

150

her husband. Behind him, standing in the kitchen door, we could see the government farmer. After a moment he turned on his heel and walked to his car. Then he drove rapidly away, and disappeared, surrounded by a cloud of dust.

Judith, still clutching the umbrella, burst into the arbor. For a second she stared helplessly around her, then she saw Elizabeth and me. She flung herself upon us, and, all three hopelessly entangled in the umbrella, we fell in an untidy heap on the ground. Kate, with Henry and his mother, transfixed by the speed of events, stood limply in the kitchen doorway as Sitting-Standing and the horse pounded into the yard again.

The man's face was black, contorted with rage, as he pulled the horse to a sliding stop. I was frankly terrified for my own hide, and wondered dismally if my last check had reached the insurance company in time. But Elizabeth was not at all disturbed. She unscrambled herself from the pile on the ground, leaving Judith and me still, it felt, inextricably attached to the umbrella, its ribs caught in our hair. Then reaching into the melee, Elizabeth seized Judith's hand and held it high, as if she were a referee at the end of a fight.

Sitting-Standing simply sat in his saddle and looked at her. Judith had taken sanctuary wisely, with the two persons in the neighborhood whom he could under no circumstances approach. Sitting-Standing bowed to the inevitable. He climbed down from his saddle, and without a backward glance entered the house. The door closed behind him with the finality of a divorce court.

Judith arose, and shook out her skirts. "That old government farmer," she observed, "all the time comin' 'round, pesterin' me 'bout his 'sperimental corn. Makes me tired."

I goggled at her. "What are you going to do?" I asked.

151

Judith shrugged, the unmistakable shrug of a woman who has got a man where she wants him. "Leave him 'lone," she declared. "He come back. You see. He get over his mad. All mens do." She closed the umbrella, which had emerged undamaged from its gymnastics, with a snap.

Sitting-Standing stayed with his first wife all that week. The government farmer's car was not visible across the creek, no matter how we strained to look for it. And on the following Monday morning, without anyone's saying a word, as far as I could tell, the horse was brought, loaded, and mounted. Solemnly, like a man who knows his rights and has asserted them, Sitting-Standing rode at a walk across the creek. A week later he returned, as usual. Tradition held us all in thrall.

CHAPTER 12

LET'S GET SOME THINGS STRAIGHT

THIS is another part of the introduction; it is a chapter made up of things that need to be said. The section that follows will contain stories intended to expand and expound on the factual points that I want to make now.

Since the days when Elizabeth and I first worked together, I have encountered representatives of many of the major Indian groups still living in this country. Beginning with the Modoc in Oregon and the Kiowa in Oklahoma my interest has spread steadily, and with it has increased my acquaintance with Indians from all parts of the United States and Alaska, and some sections of Canada and Mexico. I have a tendency—it seems to me perfectly natural—to spend more time talking and writing about the Plains tribes than the others. I knew them first and still know them best, and they have always been stimulating people to be around.

Now that I am ready to stop writing about the Plains peo-

153

ples and to discuss some of the other tribes, I think it may be a good idea to tell something about Indians generally, and a few of the factors in their lives that vary from one part of this country to another. Indians have many different cultures, according to where they live, what the weather is like, and what they can find in their environment to work with.

Every once in a while, the expression "a typical Indian" crops up in conversation or writing. After long research for the elusive creature, I have come to the conclusion that he is nonexistent and that perhaps it is just as well. Life is more interesting when it is made up of individuals than when it consists of types.

We are parts of all we have met. Indian life in this country today has been formed by the movements of history, as our own has. Therefore, a few historical facts should be mentioned as we proceed.

Prior to the coming of the white men, the North American Indians had no knowledge of the wheel—the one single trait on which all contemporary European and Euro-American cultures revolve. The Indians had no metal tools or implements, although a few groups made ornaments of copper, silver, and gold. There were no written Indian languages; no domesticated animals except dogs, although bees and turkeys had been *tamed* in two areas; and there were no cultivated fruits, although agriculture of other kinds was extensively practiced.

At the time that the white men first invaded the American continents, they encountered the tribes of the Atlantic seaboard. While some customs varied from north to south along the coast, tribal folkways generally were much alike.

The Indians of the eastern woodlands were primarily hunters, who took their meat supplies from the deer, moose, and elk they found in the forests. At the same time these Indians supplemented their meat diet with foods grown in garden plots. They raised some tobacco, "to nourish their souls," as they told the white explorers, but their major crops were corn, beans, and squashes. In fact, these three plants were cultivated everywhere in the Americas that agriculture developed. For that reason they are still known as "the American vegetable triad."

The diet of large game and garden produce was further supplemented, among the Indians of the east, by rabbits, game birds, and the fish or shellfish found in streams or along the coast. Tribes in the northern part of the area, where birch trees grew, made birchbark canoes; in the south the Indians manufactured dug-outs from cypress or cedar logs. Some dug-outs were large enough to carry several persons, and in them the Indians made trading expeditions across the Caribbean and the Gulf of Mexico.

Because the tribes between the Atlantic and the Allegheny uplift generally lived in heavily wooded country, they developed an economy based on wood and its products. Their houses were made of stakes driven into the ground and set closely together to form stockaded walls. The Iroquois and some of their neighbors lived in "long houses." These bark and rush mat covered dwellings sheltered thirty to fifty people under ridge-poled roofs. Each family had its own section of the building, its own fireplace, and its own private bunks along the walls. Family living areas were partitioned from the main room.

Many of the easterners wore clothing made of deerskin, but all the woodland tribes developed some textiles. The amount of weaving produced increased as one traveled southward in the area. The fibres used were those of linden, elm, and mulberry barks, or strands of wild hemp or spun

155

milkweed fibre. Threads were spun by rolling the fibres used between the palm of the hand and the thigh. Cloth was plaited or was woven on simple frame looms.

Brocades, laces, and gauzes were among the fabrics produced by these apparently simple methods. In the south cloth was made from strips of fur or down plucked from feathers, rolled with stronger plant fibres to make fluffy threads. Other feather cloth was made by netting; the basic fabric being fashioned from plant fibres and the feathers knotted in so that they overlay one another like shingles. These cloths were brilliantly colored and draped beautifully. They were embroidered with pearls or with shell beads, and were reserved for the greatest chiefs and their families.

The easterners made basketry from splints of ash, hickory, oak, or wild cane, and from folded sheets of birchbark. Some baskets were large enough to hold a grown man; others were small enough to wear for amulets. The baskets were painted or stamped or dyed with designs in earth and vegetable colors. Sometimes baskets were embroidered with moose hair or porcupine quills or strands of fine grasses. Also the women of the eastern tribes made rush mats, to be used as bedding or to cover the walls or roofs of the houses.

The eastern Indians also made pottery. It was moulded without the wheel, of course, but it was evenly-shaped and well-proportioned. The pottery was unglazed, and it was seldom water-proof, but it was very handsome, with its painted or incised decorations and its highly polished finish. The vessels ranged in size from toys for little girls to cooking jars big enough to hold the meat of a full-grown deer.

But the eastern Indians excelled as carvers. They carved in bone, they carved in stone, they traded with the Indians of Florida and the Bahamas for conch shells to carve, and above all they carved in wood. These sculptors worked with stone tools and wet sand to produce works of art that were monumental in character and superb in quality.

The tribes of the east were town dwellers. Their clusters of long houses or single-family dwellings were sometimes set on mounds or sometimes were surrounded with stockades as defense against prowling animals or enemy tribes. The fields, cultivated by the women, were outside the pickets but within easy reach of home in case of an emergency. Inside the palings, the towns were usually fairly clean—always cleaner than the European cities of the discovery period. There were definite latrine areas; there were dumping grounds for household rubbish, and there were the half-wild dogs that helped the crows scavenge the dump heaps and streets and keep garbage at a minimum.

These Indians were much interested in government and its problems. In general the eastern tribes traced descent through a man's mother. If he were descended from a woman of the Bear clan he was a Bear. If a Bear woman married, her children were little Bears, for children always belonged to their mother's clan. Half the clans of each tribe formed a unit, and the other half opposed them in dances, ceremonial ball games, and tribal elections. Only the son of a mother who belonged to the tribe could vote. The women could not, but they were granted the right to advise and argue. They used it so successfully that the early Europeans described these tribes as matriarchies, governed by the women.

In the southern part of the area, the tribes were controlled by small groups of men, half hereditary chiefs, half priests. In the extreme southeast an aristocracy was dominant. Here chieftainship was hereditary and was the topmost slab of a pyramid composed of slaves, freedmen, nobles, and kings. The kings were called Suns.

Our information on Indian religions is far from complete, but as far as we know that of the eastern tribes was rather like the beliefs of the ancient Greeks. The Indians endowed their surroundings with a multitude of wood spirits, water spirits, flower spirits, and animal spirits, most of them beneficent in character. In the extreme southeast a cult of death —greatly concerned with the preservation of ancestral bones and the construction of elaborate mausoleums to hold same —rose and flourished shortly before the conquest. It was a harmless sort of business, about on a par with the tomb-building of the Norman knights.

Somewhere in the east there was a dim belief in an over-all spirit for good—what the Europeans referred to as The Great Spirit. Where this personality lived we have no idea— nor do we know whether he had a designated dwelling beyond the sky or below the ground. He must have had a home somewhere, for the Great Hare and certain birds were his messengers to man, and brought man's feeble prayers back to him. But because the first settlers confused this person with the devil, we know very little about him now. We cannot say whether the Great Spirit actually maintained the Happy Hunting Ground, or whether that concept should be credited to the invaders.

Today we find the remnants of the great culture of the eastern woodlands scattered to the winds. A few tribes survived in their ancestral homes, but some were exterminated and some were removed to the west, and settled in Kansas and Oklahoma.

West of the Mississippi, the woodlands culture fringed out and finally terminated at the line of the Cross Timbers. This belt of matted, low-growing trees, lashed together with brush and vines, runs from the Gulf Coast of Texas to the Ozark uplift in central Missouri. It is a clear-cut boundary, separating the Indian cultures of the east from those of the west.

Beyond the Timbers on the west stretch the Great Plains, the rolling central grasslands of the continent. It is a region of sharp climatic variation, once carpeted with grasses, and covered with light soils that the grasses bound in place.

Before the white men came, only the buffalo herds lived the year round on the Plains. Along the margins of the grasslands the Indians cultivated patches of garden. The people lived in houses that were built half underground. We know very little of the life that went on in those houses, for they were abandoned early in recorded history. As soon as the whites arrived and turned their horses loose to graze, the Indians deserted their holes in the ground and took up a freer life.

With the first captured, stolen horses a door was opened from the house underground into the sunlight of mobility, and the Indians streamed out of their pit houses. Dwellings, clothing, household utensils, objects of art—all were made from the skins or bones of animals, sometimes supplemented with wood. What the prairie Indians could not carry with them, they abruptly discarded. Why bother? Everybody rode horseback, and loads were carried on drags made from tipi poles and slung from bone or wooden pack saddles. Everything in the Plains Indians' lives had at least two uses, and often could be made to serve for three or more.

These people were hunters and meat eaters. If the Indians found fruits, berries, or vegetables growing wild, they picked and ate them on the spot. Some women mixed plant foods in their meat dishes, but they seem to have been in a class with the gourmet cooks of today. Day in and day out the people ate meat, and it sufficed. Buffalo meat for preference, deer or antelope meat for an occasional change, ground

159

squirrel or rabbit or prairie dog meat if there were nothing else to be had. Sometimes they shot prairie chickens, sage hens, or wild turkeys, but they never bothered with the eggs. Fish from the muddy prairie streams was unappetizing at best.

The Plains Indian men shared some customs with the Knights of the Round Table. The young men formed into bands, and roamed the country to see how they might advantage themselves. There were systems of heraldry, and men's shields bore symbols of power. There was not much dying of love or vowing eternal constancy—eternal chastity was more often vowed—but there was a good deal of dwelling on love as a topic of poetry and song.

Above all the Plains Indian man sought his Holy Grail. From boyhood he went alone to the high and lonely places, or the inner depths of the canyons that slash across the plains, to find a spirit to guide and guard him throughout his life. If he were fortunate his quest was rewarded and he wore on his person or his shield a token of his good fortune.

Each Plains tribe was divided into bands, and families often counted descent through their fathers and grandfathers. An individual could hardly survive or support a family entirely alone. At the same time, too many people living too close together for any considerable period of time would exhaust the resources of game and grass. So the bands camped apart most of the year and only gathered together in a tribal camp in midsummer, the time of the Sun Dance. If a man wished to leave one band and live with another, or if he wished to leave his own tribe and ally himself with a neighboring one, he made his own decision. Should he violate the rules of the group, on the other hand, the group could visit upon him the ultimate shame and punishment— exile.

Bands were directed by chiefs, who were informally chosen from among the able-bodied and responsible men. The band chiefs of a tribe composed an informally chosen council, which usually met during the annual Sun Dance for purposes of allotting hunting areas and dealing with intertribal relations. In a few places on the Plains the institution of hereditary chieftainship was acknowledged. It would probably not have been a safe thing to suggest to those extreme individualists, the Kiowa and Comanche for instance.

Plains religion was formally expressed through the eight-day ceremony of the Sun Dance. However, the religion cannot be called sun worship, for like the religion of the woodlands peoples it was actually a pantheism. Nature spirits surrounded and protected—or, sometimes, warred upon—humanity.

Along the Rio Grande and its tributaries, north into Colorado and Utah and south into Chihuahua and Sonora, there was a well-established Indian life pattern: that of the Pueblos, or town-dwellers. These were people who lived in villages—sometimes almost cities—like the easterners. Unlike the woodland peoples, the Indians of the Pueblos had almost no wood; certainly not enough to build with. Instead, they made their houses of stones gathered from streams, from slabs of sandstone, from blocks of volcanic tufa, or from puddled mud. The walls of buildings were plastered with mud, smoothed and worked to a firm texture. After the Spaniards came and taught the Indians how to make them, mud bricks were used for building.

The Indians of the Pueblos were farmers. Besides the vegetables of the triad they raised tobacco, melons, cotton, sunflowers and giant rag weed for the edible seeds. Theirs was a country of brief, seasonal rains. Most of the moisture for the gardens came from the run-off from melting snows,

161

so the men of the Pueblos practiced dry farming. They knew the principles of land and water conservation, how to irrigate, how to plant in clumps instead of rows, and something of crop rotation, before the white men came among them.

Some men were ritually empowered to hunt for deer, antelope, or elk. The meat was only a supplement to the main diet, for whatever game was brought in must be divided among all the group. There were annual rabbit drives, some game birds were eaten, and in certain Pueblos fish from the mountain streams formed a part of the diet. The tamed turkeys that plock-tocked on the dump heaps were apparently kept more for their feathers than for their meat, as were the eagles caged and sullen on the roof-tops.

Within the walls of their apartment-house towns, while the winter fields rested, these Indians developed their arts. Basketry and textiles, pottery, and carvings were all produced. Above all, the Pueblo Indians were painters. Earth in their country was of many hues: chrome and gamboge yellows, the blue or green of volcanic muds, white from deposits of kaolin, reds from hematite cliffs, and black from the charcoal of their fires. On the walls of their houses and their underground places of worship, on their pottery, on their fabrics, on rock formations, the Pueblo Indians painted.

Religion and government were inextricably mixed in the southwestern towns, and they are still mingled today. White people who tell you what and how much they know about these matters are either violating confidences or falsifying. I do not know what it would take to induce a Pueblo Indian to discuss honestly and frankly the government and religion of his people. I do know that if I were in possession of that information I should not expect to live long if I divulged it in casual conversation to casual ears.

Hanging around the fringes of the Pueblos are a bunch of

Johnny-Come-Latelys, the Athabascans. They descended on the townsmen about three centuries before the whites, from the northwest. We know them by distortions of their Pueblo names, as Apaches and Navahos.

The peculiar genius of the Athabascans is their protective coloration. It is practically impossible now to determine what they were like to begin with, beyond the fact that they were hunters. As we and all other white men have known them, their lives and customs have been flavored with Pueblo ways. After the Spanish invasion the Athabascans became tough, wandering shepherds. Before that they were tough, wandering freebooters, who took what they wanted where they found it.

The band organization of the Athabascans seems to have remained unchanged since their earliest days, however. It was looser than that which existed on the plains. Apparently all governmental matters were managed by a committee of the whole, with a shrill fringe of women on the outskirts of the council to keep the men in line. There were no true chiefs, every man was a councilor. Families camped in groups, free to come and go as they pleased. There were no towns, and the dwellings seem to have varied from pit-houses to shelters made by slamming brush and branches together. A death in the family meant that the house was abandoned and the survivors moved on to build a new shelter elsewhere.

The Athabascans were originally hunters and fighters, consequently their great craft was weapon-making. They invented compound bows, backed with sinew, that were as efficient as many European and Asiatic cross-bows. They made short spears. Almost everything in Athabascan life seems to have been directed to making man the successful conqueror of deer, elk, large birds, and occasional antelope and buffalo—not to mention human enemies.

163

To this end boys were trained in feats of endurance that seem incredible to us today; they ran great distances, they fasted for days on end, they swam in icy water, or they lifted tremendous weights. And if the life of the Athabascan men was hard, so was that of the Athabascan women. They too trained themselves to endurance and stoicism, and passing certain tests of these qualities was part of a girl's initiation into womanhood.

The old religion of the Athabascans, if we may judge from the fragments of it that survived among the Apaches, consisted of an unlimited pantheon of spirits, most of them hostile to man and requiring placation. There were good spirits too, but they seldom caught up with the bad ones. Life was rugged, in every sense, and the life of the supernatural was as forbidding as that of the natural world.

South and west of the Pueblos, in the valleys of the Salt and Gila Rivers, lived another agricultural people. By the time the whites reached this area, their agriculture had dwindled to the growing of the triad vegetables in irrigated patches. There was some hunting. These people ate the fish they caught from the muddy, shallow waters of their country, usually cooking them whole until the flesh fell from the bones and the bones softened. Pounded wild seeds or corn were stirred into the mess, and the whole business was scooped from the pot and eaten lukewarm whenever anyone was hungry. Why the entire population did not die of botulism has not been disclosed to us.

But these people, living in small clusters of brush shelters, were artists in their own way. The women made fine pottery, and the baskets they wrought from the desert brush and grasses served them for many needs. Men *ran* from southern Arizona to the Gulf of California and back, with only the briefest of stops on the way for sleep or to swallow pinches of mesquite-bean meal. They brought back shells to carve and to trade with the Pueblo Indians.

The people of the deserts were governed by councilors who advised hereditary chiefs. Their religion was that of the world around them: the spirits of the desert and the cacti, of the mountains and the muddy rivers and the occasional trees, all of whom aided men and gave advice and information to a supreme deity. Here, if anywhere on the North American continent, a Great Spirit may be said to have existed in the minds of men.

These desert people were the tallest North Americans. The men were on an average six feet tall, and seven feet was not an impossible height for a man to reach. They fought with clubs, when they were attacked, but among themselves and to their friends they practiced peace and the good manners peaceful living requires. And wherever they were and whatever they did, like all Indians, the desert people sang. Their poetry and their chanted prayers were among the most complex in imagery and construction the Indian world knew.

North of the desert farmers, in Nevada and western Utah, and inland Oregon and Washington, the country was too harsh for agriculture of any kind. Here the people hunted large and small game, and along the rivers they fished. However, their great dependence for food was on the roots and seeds of wild plants. So much did these Indians depend on gathering wild plant foods, that the first white men who met them called them the "Digger Indians." The name has stuck to the Plateau peoples, unfortunately misused as a term of contempt, until this day.

The contempt was undeserved. Had the whites taken the trouble to find out, they would have discovered among the Indians of the Plateau many traits that were not unfamiliar to themselves. Like the tribes of the southeast, the Plateau peoples had an hereditary aristocracy based on slavery. Their chiefs and councilors were not elected, they achieved positions of authority because they belonged to certain families. They trained their successors from childhood to maturity, and a man's status in his community could often be measured by the number of wives and descendants he could afford to maintain.

The Plateau peoples did not make pottery, but they were superb basketmakers. Clothing, household utensils, bedding, and the warriors' armor, all were made of basketry. Cedar-bark and rush mats were used to increase the comfort of the pit-houses in which the people lived. In the northern part of the area, where the winters were extremely severe, the people wore skin clothing; in the southern part, where protection from the sun was chiefly needed, they often wore garments made of strips of shredded barks.

In this area, for the first time, we find Indians with an established currency. Except in California, where the life of the Indians was similar to that of the plateau, Indians had no systems of material values. Barter was the basis of all economics. But from Reno to Hollywood and north to Seattle, aboriginally, the Indians had a currency consisting of beads ground from shells. So many shell beads constituted an official finger-length, and were worth a deerskin or an obsidian blade. For convenience, many of the Plateau people had bead-measuring gauges tattooed on their forearms.

Religion in the Plateau and California tribes was systematized. There was an almost-supreme being—almost supreme because he had once been married and had fathered a son who might some day replace him. In descending order from these two deities came the ranks of an established hierarchy: war spirits, hunting spirits, and the spirits of the dead. None was to be trifled with, all required certain ceremonies to be observed in their honor. The bodies of the dead were burned, so that their spirits might escape from the world of men and enter the world of the beyond. This world was located in the heavens.

Last of the great culture areas of the present United States was the Northwest Coast. Here again we find a forest world, and here in many material ways the culture of the eastern woodlands is repeated. Great plank houses were built to shelter families and bands. There were also great plank canoes, to carry men in war and women on fishing or house-moving expeditions. Woodcarving was a highly developed art, and so was the making of basketry and of other fine textiles. There was no pottery on the northwest coast, and no agriculture was practiced in this area.

These tribes were hunters on land and fishers by sea, and their great dietary dependence was on fish and sea mammals. They caught whales. They caught the tiny olachen, or candle fish, which they dried and strung and burned to light their houses. They rendered fish oil and stored it in plank chests, to be served from bowls of carved slate at feasts. Throughout their art, in painting and carving and weaving, the forms of fish and beasts, highly conventionalized, dominate the decoration.

Religion in the northwest tribes was a rather gloomy matter. There were many evil spirits, including those of bears and of underworld dwellers who subsisted on human flesh. There were undersea monsters. There were undefined but horrible beings who haunted the woods and the sea shore.

In order to make life bearable in such a forbidding world, the northwest coast Indians worked out a series of elaborate rituals, which were almost theatrical performances. In their manner of presentation these ceremonies resembled the

167

staging of medieval miracle and morality plays. Dances were held in the community houses, with masked performers to represent the various monster spirits, who appeared through concealed openings in the carved and painted wooden screens or partitions, or emerged from holes in the floor. The dancers' costumes were rich with abalone shells and walrus ivory carvings; their masks sometimes hid only the wearers' eyes; sometimes concealed their heads and shoulders. Masks were made to open in series, like puzzle boxes, and reveal masks within masks, each more horrible than the one before it until the ultimate, inner ghastliness was reached and the dancer vanished in a flash of diabolic flame—produced by throwing fish oil on the fire.

Woodcarving was the great northwest coast art from the days when only stone and bone tools were obtainable. The early art was very fine, but after the white seamen introduced steel knives in the area, the art of the northwest-coast Indians soared to new heights. Not only houses, canoes, masks, utensils, and implements were carved. It became fashionable to carve one's family crest and genealogy on a redwood trunk—quite literally, it was the family tree—and to set this record up before one's door. It was also chic to set carved wooden posts above the graves of one's ancestors, if they could be located, or, if not, in a clump somewhere in the woods. The important thing was to let the neighbors know one *had* ancestors.

A man's place in society—whether he were slave, artisan, priest, hunter, or chief, depended on the position he inherited from his forebears. It also depended on his own efforts, for prestige must be maintained and it could be increased. The men of the northwest amassed great wealth in carvings, blankets, and shields of hammered copper, for the sole purpose of destroying their worldly goods. Only a man of tremendous wealth could be so indifferent to his riches as to waste them. There are certain parallels to this custom in our own culture.

In all these culture areas, in all this wide range of life patterns, there were, when the white men first landed on the Atlantic coast, over two hundred Indian tribes, and a population of less than a million persons. In fact the most reliable estimate available sets the population at that time as having been about four hundred thousand persons in the United States and Alaska. Each tribe had its own citizens, its own customs, its own ways of living, and its own language and literature, as I have indicated.

And the conquest and settlement of the United States was a slow process, for each tribe had to be dealt with separately, and many times over. Each of the conquering nations: Spanish, English, French, Dutch—made its own treaties with each tribe that it encountered. Because of the treaties, and the orations and discussions that were delivered over them, we have fragments of Indian poetry, humor, and political thought. In some cases these fragments are all that have been preserved of the life-stuff of a people.

Each treaty regulated Indian-white relations slightly differently. One clause that was an almost unvarying constant, though, recurred in most of them. It was that the Indians gave up land to the white men. The great variation came in the terms of what the Indians got in return for their real estate: beads, whiskey, trade goods, or schools and medical care.

For a time, in what looks like an effort to imitate Indian poetry, treaties were made to endure "as long as the grass shall grow and the rivers shall run." No greater verbal irony was ever committed to paper. Because of early ideas of soil

169

conservation, rivers rapidly ceased to run and grass to grow on vast stretches of Indian lands. Plowing and subsequent erosion took their toll of earth that was none too good to begin with. Where there had once been grass and rivers there came to be the new American desert—the dust bowl.

Indian treaties often contained provisions for "health, welfare, and education services" for members of tribes. These clauses have been interpreted as meaning anything from a one-room schoolhouse at home to a multiple-unit boarding school three thousand miles away. Health service has sometimes meant that hospitals, built and equipped at great expense, must be abandoned for lack of personnel to serve in isolated areas. Sometimes health service means a single field nurse conscientiously trying to cover five hundred miles and help five thousand people in her monthly rounds. Welfare service, too, varies widely: from barrels of old clothes shipped by home-mission societies to government funds placed at the disposal of tribal councils. In each case treaty provisions have been met and service rendered.

The question of welfare and its administration raises the further question of self-determination and its accompanying problems. The chief of these is the inaccurate, but generally held notion that all Indians everywhere are "wards of the government."

Off-hand, I cannot remember any treaty with any Indian tribe in which the term "wardship" or its related derivatives was used. There must have been one somewhere or the phrase would not have become so firmly rooted in the national language. But I do not recall it, any more than I can recollect an official government document employing the words "second-class citizens." These terms so loaded with emotional dynamite, seem to have arisen by spontaneous generation.

The very fact that the government of the United States made treaties with Indian tribes assumes that members of those tribes were judged to be sufficiently intelligent to be able to manage their own affairs. Several Indian tribes, even after the American Revolution, sent ambassadors to European governments and to Washington. Many of the southeastern tribes, notably the Cherokee, Choctaw, Chickasaw, and Creek, have been self-governing to the point of having bi-cameral legislatures, elected executive, courts of law, and written legal codes, both criminal and civil. These tribes supported schools, national newspapers and magazines, and made provision for old age assistance and aid to widows and orphans. These are not the life plans of peoples who need guardians. They are the schemes of groups who are prepared to deal with emergencies as they arise, and to deal with them capably.

It cannot be denied that many Indians, both individually and as members of tribes, suffered loss and damage at the hands of the white invaders. They were not prepared to cope with white men or the white man's world. In general, these Indians belonged to the nomadic tribes which lacked concepts of land ownership. When they were required to adjust their thinking to an economic pattern that depended entirely on personal ownership of land, the effort was sometimes too great for the Indians to make.

No one has ever decided exactly why the reservation system was established. Nowadays it is fashionable to refer to it has having been instituted "for the protection of the Indians." Unfortunately, a thorough reading of American history suggests that the original beneficiaries of the reservation enclosure of Indians were intended to be the whites who were homesteading on Indian lands. The intruders were to be protected against the marauding aboriginal owners of the real estate by strong fences and the military.

171

In time the system naturally worked both ways, as things usually do. The Indians were handed certain tracts of land— often portions of their original territory—and were told to stay on them as long as the grass and the rivers followed the regular course of nature. They were also assured that for an equally protracted period whites would be kept off the Indians' lands.

During the years of reservation establishment, the Indians were members of tribes either hostile to or under treaty agreements with the United States government. It is important to keep that fact in mind. They were no more voting citizens of the United States than are members of the French consular service—and for exactly the same reason. Their lands formed isolated but actual portions of ground belonging to other governments, of which they were citizens.

In recent years what are called "Jurisdictions" have been created to replace reservations. The differences between the two today are largely in name only. In most cases reservations and jurisdictions are similarly administered. Jurisdiction has a softer sound than reservation, and Indians generally prefer to use it, as more dignified and self-respecting.

I don't believe that it occurred to any Indians in the early days to resent their lack of United States franchise. I don't believe they thought of wanting the franchise. They were vigorously employed in avoiding or evading the representatives of that government, and as for voting in local or national elections, the Indians probably never thought of it.

And I also believe that at the root of many of today's "Indian problems" one may still find this single, simple, political fact: Indians aren't used to thinking of themselves as part of the United States, but as parts of their own tribes.

At the time when the voting question first arose in regard to Indians, the franchise was a most important part of white American thinking. The Civil War had been fought, in part, over the extension of the vote to the Negro population. Women were raising their family roofs to obtain the right to vote. There was even an extreme movement in some states to abolish the poll tax and property and literacy qualifications for voters. Everybody else wanted to vote and to vote freely; if the Indians were as smart as their friends said they were, they would want to vote too.

After the first World War, in recognition of the military service of the Indian men, the *national* franchise was extended to all Indians in the United States and its territories.

And here an often-forgotten fact should be mentioned. The nation may grant the franchise to a given group, but each state qualifies its own voters. Some states have strict regulations about payment of poll taxes, passage of literacy tests, or possession of grandparents who could have passed literacy tests but who are dead and can't be produced in proof. All such requirements have been held unconstitutional at various times, but they continue to be operative.

So, while after 1924 all Indians over twenty-one *could* vote in national elections, they didn't, because of state-created hurdles to enfranchisement. Not until 1947 did the last states—Arizona and New Mexico—grant Indians the right to qualify as voters in all elections.

That is one major problem set forth in as simple language as possible. Accompanying it is another. It is often said that no Indians are allowed to own their own lands. And no Indians—it is also asserted—pay taxes.

The question of taxation is the simpler one to answer. Let's take it first. Indians don't pay taxes on lands guaranteed to them under tribal treaties. This tax exemption is similar to that operative on homesteaded lands owned by

173

whites. The land is not taxed in the case of holders of home-stead exemptions, but improvements on the land are: pave-ments, municipal sewage and garbage collections, light and power franchises, municipal transportation lines, and the like, all mean the levying of taxes on land-owners. The farther out in the country people live, the less land improve-ment tax they pay. Indians, who usually live beyond all land improvements except those guaranteed to them by treaty provisions don't pay taxes on improvements.

But if an Indian moves to town, as he is perfectly free to do if he wants to, and buys a piece of land there, he pays taxes on it. Indians also pay sales taxes, automobile taxes, federal luxury taxes, and tobacco taxes, not to mention income taxes. Don't ever let anybody tell you that Indians as a group are tax-exempt.

The question of sale or leasing of Indian lands simply cannot be dealt with in general terms. All the endless com-plications and misunderstandings, all the misapprehensions and misinformation on the subject, seem to have come from efforts to generalize. Because each tribe was a separate entity to begin with, and because each tribe made its own treaties with the United States, there are as many answers to the questions of Indian land ownership as there are tribes. More. There are as many answers as there are treaties.

The great central problem hinges on the question of how the lands were certified to a given tribe in a given treaty. Lands were certified to *each tribe as a whole,* or to *the members of given tribes in common,* or to *the members of tribes in severalty* (as individual owners).

Now, every time the government lawyers think they have the problems of any given tribe straightened out and ex-plained to their own satisfaction, some bright tribesman turns up another treaty and hires another attorney, and the

174

whole thing has to be gone into all over again. No one can yet foresee the end of all this.

As an encouragement to the Indians and their friends, however, the trend of national thinking now is in the direction of giving each Indian *who wants it* a tract of land that he can dispose of to suit himself. Not all Indians want to own their own farms or city lots, and some, if they were offered ownership of property, would refuse the gift. But unless the law suits now in the courts and those which can be expected to arise from them are prolonged unduly, it can be predicted that every Indian who wants a farm should own it by about 2050.

By that time the Indian population of the United States will probably have increased at about the same rate it has for the last fifty years, almost twice the rate of increase of the general population. The general population will have materially declined, following its steady tendency. The percentage and absolute of fullblood Indians to general population is steadily rising. Within that hundred years or so the country will have handed itself back to the Indians.

The last general topic I am going to deal with here is the United States Indian Service. It can best be defined as that Civil Service body which takes the worst kicking around from the largest number of people—including its own employees—in the country. Always excepting the State Department.

The Indian Service exercises many functions. It directs health, welfare, and educational services among all Indians and tribes of Indians. The services include soil, water, and timber conservation, preservation of other natural resources, development of livestock and crafts production, swamp drainage, road building, dental, medical, and nursing care, arbitration of family disputes, dealing with endless legal arguments, teaching little girls to darn and little boys to feed chickens and both to brush their teeth, and assisting housewives with canning.

The Indian Service is staffed entirely by human beings. They make mistakes. They like some people better than others, and they sometimes show it. They dislike bad roads and hard work and isolation. Sometimes they get bored with Indian dances and the prolongation of council meetings. But they make their livings by putting up with things they don't like and making the best of those they do, just like the rest of us.

The Indian Service operates under authority granted by Acts of Congress, and it receives its operating funds from Congressional appropriations, like the Post Office and Treasury Departments. When an appropriation bill is up for consideration, it is at the mercy of congressmen, like any other appropriation bill. If an Indian voter in the backwoods of Wyoming is annoyed with the activities of local Indian Service employees, he can write to his congressman like any other voter, and the inevitable can happen.

The Indian Service can be made to sound paternalistic and anachronistic and wasteful and useless by its enemies. It can also be made to sound like an ideal administrative device by its defenders. Actually, it is only as useful and as useless as the Civil Service system that lies behind it.

But the Indian Service, for the last twenty years, has been unobtrusively and gradually working itself out of a job. Able and qualified Indian candidates for the Indian Service receive preference over all others. Unfortunately, government salaries are not the best to be had in this country. Frequently a qualified Indian: teacher, administrator, attorney, social worker, physician, dentist, or nurse, can make more money competitively in the white man's world than he can in government service.

How do Indians generally make their livings? Exactly as other people do. The government does not pay them for existing. Those who are qualified by old age, ill health, or misfortune, draw state welfare benefits as whites and Negroes do. Indians, nowadays, are citizens of the United States, and they take the bitter with the sweet as all the rest of us must.

CHAPTER 13

GAINFUL EMPLOYMENT

Some time ago I indicated that employment is a problem in an ethnologist's life. The choice of position usually lies between teaching in a university and becoming a museum curator. To do either a union card in the form of a Ph.D. is necessary.

Anthropology generally is a man's trade, and women have a time fitting themselves into it. Unless a woman has been endowed by nature with tremendous health, enthusiasm, and drive, she does not get to the top. I don't want to sound unhappy about the matter—after all, some of my best friends and closest allies are men. But the fact remains that to get anywhere as an anthropologist a woman must work twice as hard and be twice as good as any of the several men available to take her place. And she *still* needs that Ph.D.

The time came when I was faced with the decision as to which of several universities should receive the honor of bestowing my Ph.D. While I was still shopping around, weighing available scholarship funds against location and both against congenial faculty personnel, I had a phone call from a stranger.

"I'm working for the Indian Arts and Crafts Board," said an agreeable female voice at the other end of the line. "I hear you know something about the Kiowa. I wonder if I could talk to you?"

I met the owner of the voice that evening for dinner, and we talked considerably. Before I went home, I looked over and finally put into my purse the Civil Service application forms for a job as a Specialist in Indian Arts and Crafts. The next morning I filled them out and mailed them to Washington. I then forgot all about the matter, and resumed my game of button-button-who's-got-the-button with the universities.

I never was more shocked in my life than when the telegram arrived informing me that I had been on the payroll of the Indian Arts and Crafts Board for three days, and instructing me to go back to the Kiowa and get to work on a study of their material culture. I carried it downstairs from the laboratory and showed it to the professor.

"That's nice," he observed. "What are you waiting for?"

"Well—" I said. "I don't know anything about it—"

"You're working for it, aren't you? How does it happen you got a job that you don't know anything about?"

"Well, the woman said they were going to make an intensive study of Indian arts and crafts with an idea to encouraging production and marketing. They think that Indian arts can be sold if they can be produced in quantity and made available on the wider market instead of just selling trash for a quarter a throw on railroad-station platforms and in souvenir shops—"

"I guess you've got the general idea," the professor remarked. "What about that Ph.D. you've been kicking around, though?"

"Well—well—well—it's an awfully good salary—better than I could get anywhere else—and I thought if I worked a couple of years and saved my money I could go back to graduate school. The Department of the Interior will grant educational leaves for things like that, she said."

"It might be a good notion at that," the professor said as he hoisted his feet onto the top of his desk and fished a cigarette from the pack in his shirt pocket. "Especially since they've got the sense to send you back to the Kiowa. Keep careful notes as you go along, and you may get your dissertation out of it. After all, there is no adequate study of the material culture of a southern Plains tribe."

By the time a week later when my official notice of appointment arrived, I was back where I felt most at home, hounding Mrs. Camp and Grandmother and the old uncle for all they could remember about hide-tanning and beadwork and weapon-making. Systematically all the details of material culture went into my notebook and came out again by way of the typewriter, and a pile of information began to accumulate. I dutifully sent the week's clutch off to Washington every Saturday noon, and continued to enjoy myself. Best of all, I was getting not only my expenses, but a salary, for doing what I loved best in all the world.

Long before I felt I had exhausted the subject of Kiowa material culture, I was "pulled out" as I learned to call it, and sent somewhere else. Before being sent I was summoned to the central office for examination and briefing.

"I'm afraid this won't be as easy a job as the Kiowa," said the Board's general manager by way of an entering wedge. "We need some information on the Oklahoma Choctaw.

According to the report of the Regional Director of the Indian Service, they're having a pretty hard time. The annual income per family is forty-nine dollars and fifty cents, and the county where they live is remote and too poor to support a large WPA project. It may be an opportunity for us to accomplish something concrete."

"What do you have in mind?" I asked, automatically opening my notebook.

"Several things, ultimately," declared the general manager. "First, I think you ought to go down to the southeast part of the state and talk to the Indian Service social worker. She knows more about the people, what they can do and would like to do, than anyone else. Take any suggestions and help you can get from her, and write us a preliminary report."

"What do you want me to report on?"

"She says," said the general manager, "that some of the women down there can make baskets. Go and find out what kind of baskets they can make. See if they're good and strong and durable; see if they could be used for market baskets or fishing creels or something. See what they're made of and how and if the people who make them use vegetable or commercial dyes. Get all the dope you can about baskets —and keep your eyes open. There may be something else that the social worker hasn't mentioned in her reports. Here they are. See if you can supplement them with specialized information."

The trip to the Choctaw country involved springtime and blossoming meadows and flowering redbud and dogwood trees. It also involved sluggish, slow-moving streams, and bayous where the rivers had overflowed, and sloughs where mosquitoes were breeding busily. I stopped for quinine at

181

the next town, and from that time on I floated four inches above the ground in a humming haze. But I missed another bout of malaria, and that was all I cared about.

The social worker was Choctaw herself. She belonged in this county where she had been born and had grown up. She knew every backwoods trail and sand road, she spoke Choctaw. We went from one log cabin—smoke curling from wattle-daub chimneys—to another, visiting and talking and meeting the basketmakers.

The baskets were fine as far as they went. They were made of local wild cane splints, dyed with walnut bark and puccoon root and apple bark and pokeberry juice. They were made for home use, they were utilitarian and strong and functionally handsome as things made for use generally are. But they were too good. A basket would last a Choctaw woman a lifetime if she used it carefully, and the six available basketmakers were more than able to keep up with tribal demand and also supply a limited outside market. And a limited market was the best we could expect.

All the same, it was apparent that the Choctaw women needed help of some kind and needed it badly. Log cabins with wattle-daub chimneys are extremely picturesque. They are also, I soon discovered, damp (especially when they have earth floors), grimy (because the chimneys leak smoke and soot into the rooms), cramped as far as accommodations go (because they are often one-roomed), and dark (because they lacked windows and sometimes the weather did not permit keeping doors open).

The people who lived in the cabins were, the social worker told me and I could see for myself, far from well. The field nurse talked of cases of pellagra and hookworm; malaria and its ravages were visible to anyone's eye. There were some cases of tuberculosis who could not be cared for in an already crowded sanitorium. Just plain old-fashioned hunger was there, too. This year's crops were in but not up, and last year's harvest was almost exhausted. It was a pitiable situation, faced, on every hand, with courage and dignity.

Then came a day when the social worker took me to a cabin that was more prosperous than the average. It had two windows and a porch. On the porch stood a huge old spinning wheel, designed for making cotton thread. I admired it.

"She spins wool," the social worker informed me. "She and her sisters have three sheep, and they make yarn for sweaters and stockings."

In fact, our hostess wore a sweater of her own spinning and knitting while we talked to her. Because I had been told to mention *any* other craft, I included the three spinners in my report.

From that time on, matters progressed at a speed that left me breathless. I was informed by the general manager that while the world was full of hand weavers, they frequently lacked hand-spun yarns to work with. Here was the very thing we were looking for: a product with an almost unlimited market. As for potential production, there were three hundred women available. Surely as many as wanted to could learn to spin. They could be organized into a production and marketing cooperative. Yarn could be sold. The proceeds could be invested in more wool for more spinning and in payment of the spinners. It was all beautifully simple, except for the matter of teaching spinning.

The general manager consulted the Education Division of the Indian Service. The Education Division supplied a teacher. Equipped with a car, four spinning wheels, and a hundred pounds of raw wool, she disappeared into the Choctaw country. My instructions were to work with her when she expressed a need for help; otherwise to go on about my business organizing the Plains tribes into a beadwork cooperative and leave well enough alone.

Two months later I received a letter from the spinning teacher.

"I think you had better come down here," she wrote. "We have some yarn spun and lots of the women want to work, but we are out of wool and spinning wheels."

I abandoned the Plains people to their endless argument about whether beads could be sewn on moccasins best with linen thread or sinew, and departed for the southeast. It would be a month or more before the linen thread was disposed of. I was determined it should not be used, and so were the most expert beadworkers, but only time and local social pressure would produce results. It was an excellent opportunity to visit the Choctaw project.

The spinning teacher got me up at six the morning after I arrived.

"They like to go to work early," she explained.

We drove across country to a church, unused in the middle of the week. A woman, clean and fresh and hopeful of face, came across the clearing and unlocked the door. The puncheon floor was swept clean, and on it stood three spinning wheels, newly made, whittled from local second-growth walnut with jackknives. "The men could do better if they had some wood-worker tools," the teacher remarked.

We carried another four wheels from the car and set them up. More women appeared. By eight o'clock the room hummed with activity. Women carded into rolls the wool that the children picked and shook clean. Other women, taking turns at the wheels, spun the rolls into yarn. The spinners moved backwards and forwards and the wheels sang for their dancing all morning long. At the end of each hour, the groups changed places, so that everyone had a chance to spin.

I sat and cleaned wool and watched. The teacher moved about easily, watching, guiding, somehow instructing. She spoke no Choctaw and only a few women spoke a little English, but somehow they communicated with each other. We stopped for lunch at noon, sharing sandwiches and coffee from the car with the others and receiving our shares of boiled pork and hominy. So it went on all day, until late afternoon. Then the work was gathered up and loaded into the car with the wheels, the floor was swept, and as silently as they had gathered the women slipped away into the woods.

That night we sat late in our tourist-court room grading the yarn. Some of it was smooth and even and strong. But most of it was lumpy and irregular, and showed the results of struggles with new motion patterns and unfamiliar materials.

"I don't know what to do with this kind," the teacher said, showing me a particular knotty strand. "It's strong; I don't know what you'd have to do to break it. And I don't want to discourage them by throwing *any* of it away; they've all worked so hard and they're counting so much on getting just a little bit of money from it."

"Let me take it," I suggested. "I haven't any ideas now, but maybe someone will get one."

My report after that trip was enthusiastic. Too enthusiastic. I received an immediate reply from the general manager. "We have an order for yarn," he wrote. "Ship as much as you can, immediately. It is to be used for experimental work. An artist I know wishes to produce tapestry, using the designs of modern painters in the fabrics, and would like to use hand-spun yarn for it."

185

I got out the current supply of hand-spun yarn and examined it. Much of it was worse than I remembered; it would never do for weaving; it was strong, but it would not produce a smooth, even fabric. And then—tapestry! Weavers of tapestries are much concerned with textured surfaces. Perhaps, just possibly—I hurriedly tied labels on the hanks of yarn. "Special, texture yarn for tapestry weaving," I wrote in my fanciest hand, and below, in larger letters, "Choctaw Weavers' Cooperative." With prayer in my heart and my fingers crossed, I packed and mailed the wool. After it I sent a letter. Would the weaver please, please, let us know if the yarn were suitable? If there were any in the shipment that she could use, I would bill her for that amount.

The answer came at the end of an endless week. "Please send me all you can of the special tapestry yarn—" The Choctaw spinners were on their way, and from that day to this they have never faltered. By the end of their second year the average family income per annum had increased four hundred percent. More women and more women were learning to spin and were producing. Houses had windows and around them small fields were fenced to pen the family sheep at night. And in one of the community houses was a set of woodworking tools for the men to use in making spinning wheels and tables and chairs and benches—and even, in final luxury, beds for home use. Right now I have in my closet a suit woven from Choctaw yarn by a Cherokee craftsman.

The Choctaw project was only one of many. The Indian Arts and Crafts Board boasted four field workers: one liason man who worked out of the Washington office, and three workers assigned to the Sioux, the Papago, and the Oklahoma tribes. Among us, we covered an extensive range of territory and tribes. Production began to pick up all over the map.

However, as a government agency, the Board was not allowed to advertise, directly. The Indian cooperatives which were organized for production and marketing, could not afford extensive advertising. If we were to reach the national market that was necessary to absorb the continuing production, some means of informing the public of our work was needed. The San Francisco World's Fair of 1939 finally provided the means. The Indian Arts and Crafts Board worked with Indian communities to present an exhibition of Indian crafts: the majestic antiques housed in museums all over the country and the contemporary products that were descended from them. And in connection with the exhibition, the Board assisted a California Indian community in the operation of a market for contemporary Indian crafts, in which skilled craftsmen demonstrated their working methods, and in which the best of Indian work was for sale.

In the seven years between 1936 and 1943, the Board worked hard. The Indians worked harder. When a war-induced pause occurred and there was time for stock-taking, Indian arts were on sale in internationally famous shops in many parts of the country. As nearly as we could estimate, the Indians were doing a two million dollar a year business in fine arts—instead of twenty thousand a year in curios.

Taking even a small part in this program was a full-time job, absorbing, thoroughly delightful. I didn't get the Ph.D. on educational leave. I was too afraid of missing something to stop work for a year or two. Even during a month's annual leave I was apt to feel panicky, and to suspect that I was being deprived of some excitement.

I still have the Kiowa material culture notes—increased, enriched, and supplemented with other material from the southern Plains. Maybe, some day—when I don't feel that I might miss something by not being around in Indian country, where things are really going on—maybe, when I'm really old and gray I'll get that Ph.D. yet.

CHAPTER 14

FROM OUT THE DARK PAST

O NE of my first assignments as a government ethnologist was to work with a Cherokee group in eastern Oklahoma, in order to discover if there were still any craftsmen among them. More than a hundred years before most of the great Cherokee nation surrendered their lands in western Tennessee and North Carolina and northeastern Georgia, and moved westward over what came to be known as The Trail of Tears. A few die-hards hid out in the southern Appalachians and clung to the remnants of their old territory, but the bulk of the Cherokees were relocated in two or three years between the Illinois River and the Cross Timbers, the woodland belt which divides eastern and western Oklahoma.

In the better than a century that had elapsed since their removal, these Indians had experienced the best and the worst of tribal self-government. They had remained an independent nation until 1907, when the state of Oklahoma was admitted to the Union. Then for a time they became subjects—not yet entirely citizens—of the United States.

Some Cherokees went to college, became leaders in professions and politics, and became wealthy. Others were merchants, or prosperous farmers, or pleasant, socially minded housewives.

But the group with which I was assigned to work fell into none of these "progressive" categories. Their grandparents and greatgrandparents had come from the remote, hillside, up-stream towns of the Smokies, and were best described in their own day as Indian hillbillies. The descendants of these old settlers had been located on the Oklahoma equivalents of the ancestral lands. They were out of the world and out of touch with it when I went there. Also, they were descended from the only southern Indians who had sided with the Union during the War Between the States. They were not regarded as socially desirable by the other Cherokees, and they certainly were not blessed with an abundance of this world's goods at the time of our meeting.

In preparation for the encounter I read the Bureau of American Ethnology reports on the Cherokee, and was not especially surprised to discover that the most comprehensive of them had been written by my old friend Dr. Mooney. I was growing used to having him half a century ahead of me wherever I went. I soaked up what I could of his work during the course of an afternoon.

Dr. Mooney informed me that the Cherokees were Iroquoian-speaking and had probably not been in the south very long at the time of the European discovery. He stated that they had maintained not only a northern language, but many northern customs. Their basketry, their use of masks, their social organization, their use of wampum belts, all showed strong northern influence, although their religion— probably taken over from the Creeks—was as definitely southern in origin. (More recent research has reversed this

190

information. The Cherokees and their Iroquoian cousins are now believed to be of southern origin.)

I closed the volume and considered the report without quite finishing it. Dr. Mooney was not a man to be taken lightly, nor one to use words loosely and carelessly. But still, wampum—! I had grown accustomed, although not entirely hardened, to hearing white people apply the word "wampum" to any string of beads ever owned by an Indian. I should have known Dr. Mooney better. I should have trusted him.

"Wampum" actually is only one kind of bead, and a very special one at that. Wampum was ground from the core of a particular sort of shell by the Indians of New York and New England in the days before the conquest. The shells were either transluscent blue white or an intense, dark, purplish blue in color, and they were very hard.

Grinding the beads out by hand with sandstone and sharp, wet, sand-dipped splinters of wood for tools was such a chore that the eastern Indians prized wampum above all other materials. A string of wampum beads became a symbol of truth and good faith among them. Strings—or on great occasions belts—of wampum were exchanged between tribal leaders to confirm and conclude treaties or other solemn inter-tribal agreements.

Later, the white men, beholding the reverence with which wampum was regarded by the Indians, decided that it must be a form of aboriginal currency. They set up factories in New York and New Jersey and Massachusetts, and ground wampum out by machine and by the ton. They used it not only as a medium of exchange in trading with the Indians but in their own business transactions. Production continued into the early nineteenth century, by which time the wampum market was flooded and the Indians had learned to

191

use money anyway. There were few treaties to be signed, and seeing how the whites regarded those, the Indians were not inclined to waste wampum on the signing.

But the Cherokee country had been out of the wampum region, and while pre-conquest inter-tribal trade was a good deal more extensive than is generally realized, it seemed unlikely that the Cherokees would have got their hands on much wampum. The beads were heavy, and they would have been clumsy to carry either on one's back or in a canoe. No, I eventually decided, Dr. Mooney was making the common mistake. The Cherokees must have had some shell beads, like all other southern Indians. The good doctor was mis-using the word "wampum," like many whites before and after him.

Feeling that my knowledge of the Cherokee at the turn of the century was sufficient, I set out by car to discover for myself their present condition. As I drove eastward the country sloped down and down, headed for the Mississippi in its own good geologic time. The earth became blacker and progressively soggier. I looked at the swamps that bordered the rivers I crossed and which sometimes edged the road, and I decided that I was heading right back into malarial country. The thought was depressing and I stopped and bought quinine in the next town.

A town, much further on, where I stayed, was a few miles from the Cherokee community I had set out to visit. It was spring embowered, and my hotel room was redolent of syringia and the honeysuckle and half-wild white roses that twined the porch pillars and ran along the porch roof below my window. There was more than half a moon and its light was as white as the blossoms.

Moonlight and flowers were the preparation for the enchanted world into which I drove the following morning.

Back from the highway the country rounded gently, in softly, graciously curving hills and streams. The oaks and hickories and pecans and sweet gum trees diffused the light through small leaves of differing soft greens. The log cabins along the road were well repaired and were set in clearings where the native trees had been replaced with fruit-bearing kinds. Dogwood and redbud had ceased to bloom some weeks before, yet that light through the woods suggested that a few late bloomers might still be there, out of sight, barely beyond the range of vision.

The woods were not completely silent; woods never are. There are always sounds beyond the limit of our hearing, and if we are used to woods we are aware the sounds must be there. So it was with me there along the Illinois. I did not quite hear the squirrel scratch the bark as he ran up a pecan trunk; I did not know the exact sound made by the rabbit that skittered through the fallen gum leaves when I stopped the car before the cabin of the town chief. But sounds were there—the small things of the woods had made them—and it was my misfortune that I could not hear.

The town chief was a man past middle age, and of enormous dignity in spite of his soup-bowl haircut and his overalls. We spoke at first through his son as interpreter. That was fitting, the representatives of different governments—as, in a sense, we were—should not immediately rush into personal relationships. After a time the chief discarded his own language and the interpreter. He spoke excellent English, and once the formalities had been observed we did very well without a third party.

"You say you work with Indian arts and crafts?" was his first question in English, and when I nodded, he continued, "I don't think we do any kind of craftswork here. You tell me what you mean, so maybe I'll know better. We aren't carpenters, and the young men who learn mechanics from the Indian schools get jobs in town, generally."

"I was thinking more of women's crafts," I explained. "The women are at home all the day. Maybe they do some kind of work they could sell for pin money, and we can help them find the people who will want to buy it."

The chief—Chief Dick—considered the suggestion. "Well," he remarked, "the women folks do canning and quilting, of course. Is that what you were thinking of?"

Fresh from the Plains, I answered, "Not so much those. White women do canning and quilting. I was thinking of something more Indian—oh, like beadwork or baskets or things like those."

"My grand mammy used to make baskets," Chief Dick meditated. "I never knew of any of the ladies here to do beadwork. I tell you what," he said, brightening. "My sister is the leader for all the women. We call her our Beloved Woman. She is responsible for them, and she directs them in the ceremonies. Why don't you go talk to her?"

Chief Dick gave me directions for finding his sister's home. He referred to her as Old Lady Susy, but as soon as I met her I realized that the Old Lady must be a title of respect, for she was no more than middle-aged. Old Lady Susy was as tall as her brother, a head taller than I, and she had his same great dignity and accomplished English. I explained to her, without an interpreter, what my plan was. She was immediately interested and responsive.

"I tell you what," she said at last, "this is a good time to come here. Day after tomorrow we have the full-moon dance, and everybody in the tribe will be there. I think you ought to stay and see the dance and meet the ladies. Meantime we'll go around and look up some of the older ones. It's the right time of year. They've finished the winter quilting and the strawberries won't ripen for canning for another two weeks. They have their gardens in, and except for taking care of them, the women haven't much to do now. They'll be glad to visit, and if we find anybody who still knows how to make baskets, she will have plenty of time to talk to you."

For two days we visited the clean, well-tended Cherokee homes and the women who lived in them. As a whole, the group seemed prosperous as farm prosperity goes in the spring. Old Lady Susy explained that they followed a plan their grandparents had brought west with them. Each family had its own home and garden. Widows and elderly people were assisted by the younger men; the younger women helped them with their canning and also put up supplies of vegetables and meat for use in preparing school lunches during the fall and winter. There were community corn fields and community livestock, and each man who could contributed a day a week to their care. "We all share with each other," Old Lady Susy said. "If we do find someone who can make baskets, she'll be glad to teach the others, especially if she's an old lady and hasn't any other way of sharing."

For the whole two days we searched for a basketmaker, or a weaver, or a spinster. No craftsworker was forthcoming. Dr. Mooney surged from my subconscious to my consciousness, and again I asked about beadworkers. No beadworkers. "Our Cherokee tribe never did do any beadwork."

I knew the statement was not strictly accurate, for beadwork in native shell beads and fresh-water pearls had been taken by archaeologists from known prehistoric Cherokee town-sites. But if the mists of the past had obscured the craft, there was no point in argument. I must accept the statement of the town chief and the Beloved Woman. The

Cherokees were not now, and within living memory never had been, beadworkers.

On the day of the full moon I checked out of the hotel, and left the perfumed room behind me. Old Lady Susy had offered me a place in her home until the ceremony was over. Attending the ceremony was to some extent self-indulgence. I had actually accomplished, negatively, what I had come for. But the town chief and his sister expected me to stay for the dance, and it certainly would be an opportunity to meet the people who belonged to the town.

The dance was held in a great clearing in the woods. Long, long before trees had been cut down to make an area roughly the size of a football field. Seven small, shake-roofed shelters, which the Cherokees called "beds," but which were actually open-sided lean-tos, bordered the dance grounds, and Old Lady Susy led me to the one that belonged to her clan. She saw me settled on a heap of home-made quilts, and left me there in the dusk while she went to attend to her ritual duties.

Before me, in the center of the clearing, was a pyramidal mound, and from its crest a thin feather of smoke trailed lazily against the last of the sunset. I could catch a whiff of the incense of smouldering hickory once in a while. The growing dark quivered with living presence; I heard the rustle of women's starched cotton dresses and the squeak of men's new shoes. Some people went past the shelter where I sat and were consumed by the darkness; others settled themselves around me, murmured good evenings, and were silent and waiting as I was.

We heard the shrilling of an elm-bark whistle, the thud of a drum, and the rattle of pebbles against the shells of land tortoises tied to the dancers' legs. The fire became a flame, and silhouetted against it, wrapped in the blue smoke on the top of the mound, I saw the town chief. His arms were raised full stretch above the eagle feather that was bound to the back of his head, and the call he uttered, to gather the people's attention, was that of his clan totem, the wolf.

We were back of the days of which Dr. Mooney wrote, back far beyond the knowledge of any white man. The man on the mound was transfigured, no longer a friendly, kindly soul who spoke fluent English and worried about the non-existence of beadwork, but a being in direct communication with his gods, an intermediary from them to ordinary men. And the long, half-spoken, half-sung prayer he uttered must have put him even closer to the gods than he had been when the sun sank.

Other men prayed afterwards. The Beloved Woman, standing at the foot of the mound, her arms opened wide to embrace all listening humanity, also prayed. But no prayer was so directed, none gave such immediacy of unearthly presence, as the one with which the town chief began the ceremony.

The chanting voices were silenced, then, and there was a long pause before the drum and whistle spoke again. The pebbles rattled briskly and a double file of dancers, men and women, led by a young woman, circled from the dark around the light of the fire.

The pounding of the drum and the lighter tapping of the rattles continued their obligato to the singing all the night. Moonlight and firelight met without mingling, and the sounds of the woods underlay the sound of human voices as the wood scents under ran the fragrance of the smoke. Sometimes I was keenly awake and sometimes I dozed. Once a young man stood before me, holding out his hand, and Old Lady Susy said from the darkness near me, "Go on and dance with him. We all want you to." We circled the

197

fire. Half-hypnotized by sound and scent and light and movement in the darkness, I followed the rhythm, and was told afterward that I held to it. My partner took me back to my place at the end of the song and I subsided on the quilts beside the Beloved Woman and doze-dreamed again.

I roused with daylight, to see the last dancers raise their arms in salute to the chief. He was on top of the mound again, and his upraised open palms summoned the sun forth from the folds of the hills behind us. The sun's light quenched the night's different glows, and we stumbled home along the woods path to breakfast and bed.

It was noon when I woke again. Everyone else in the family was asleep, with the exception of Old Lady Susy. She caught my eye and pointed to the wash basin in the corner of the room. When my face was fresh and my hair combed, she led me outside. We ate sitting under a hickory tree. Then I was ready to go.

"My brother said to tell you," the Beloved Woman said as we shook hands, "that he would be right obliged if you'd come by his house on your way out of town today. He has something he wants to tell you, or maybe show you—anyway, he wants you to come."

"I want to go by his place and say good-bye," I agreed. "I am very lucky to have been here with you and to have seen the ceremony."

"We don't invite very many people," Old Lady Susy observed as she followed me down the path to my car, "and I don't know when we've had a government worker here." She laughed a little. "We never had one dance with us before," she added. "We'll never forget you and we'll always welcome you for that."

She stood before her cabin, waving, and I could see her, still with her arm raised, reflected in the car mirror until I turned a bend in the road and she was finally lost to my sight.

The town chief sat before his house on a stump, evidently waiting for me. "Did you have a good time last night?" he asked like any gracious host.

"Yes," I said, "I did. A wonderful time. I don't feel tired a bit, either. Your sister said you wanted to tell me something."

"You got plenty of time?" he asked a little doubtfully. "White people always seem to Indians to be in a big hurry. This may take a while; it may take most of the afternoon."

"I've got time," I said, wondering.

He climbed into the car, and motioned me to the driver's seat.

"Let's go over to the dance ground," he said.

Smoke still curled from the peak of the mound when I parked the car in the shade of a great oak. Now in the daylight I could see that it was not a mound of earth, but a mound of ashes, blue gray and powdery, densely stacked.

"That fire never goes out," said Chief Dick. "It's been burning here in this clearing for more than a hundred years, and my grandmammy's daddy kept it burning in a brass kettle all the way across on the Trail of Tears."

He got out of the car, and I followed him along the edge of the great sun-drenched opening in the woods, to a shed that was built in a corner of the dance grounds. I had not noticed it in the dusk the night before. As we drew near the building I saw that its door was closed and padlocked. A bench stood in the shade not far away.

"You stay here," the chief instructed when we reached the bench. "We keep the clubs for the men's ball game in there, and women aren't allowed near them. We don't ever let women touch them, for fear they'll spoil the men's power.

199

The men can't go near women, or even eat food women have cooked, for four days before the game."

I sat on the bench and waited, while he produced a key from his pocket and unlocked the door. He vanished inside the shed, and I waited again. After minutes he came out, carrying a cloth-wrapped bundle which he set on the ground beside him while he made sure the door was once more securely fastened. Then, carrying the bundle, the chief returned to the bench and seated himself beside me.

"All the time we were talking, the other day," Chief Dick began, "I was trying to remember something. There was something I knew in the back of my mind, but I couldn't put my finger on it. Then, last night, when I was praying, it came back to me.

"You kept asking about beadwork, and I told you we didn't have any beadwork. It was true. As far as I know, or anybody living knows, our tribe never did make any. But I was sure there had been some beads. And last night I remembered." He stooped, and lifted the bundle to the bench between us. Evidently it was very heavy.

"When my grandmammy's daddy brought the fire from Georgia, he brought something else," the chief continued. "Long time ago, before they ever heard of the white men, the Cherokees were fighting with the Senecas. They were cousin tribes, but they were fighting. Then they saw that was wrong, and they stopped. When they smoked a pipe and made peace, the Senecas gave the Cherokees a present. They gave them beads, and they said the peace was to last forever, and the beads were the sign of it because this kind of beads never spoils.

"So I remembered that, and that my grandmammy used to keep the beads in the shed here, with the ball clubs, because she said they were sacred. Then she died, when I was about ten, and we had a spell of hard times. My daddy was town chief, and I guess he was so busy scratching to keep the people together he kind of forgot. Anyway, as far as I know, nobody's had this bundle out and looked at the beadwork since grandmammy died. I thought maybe, since you're interested in beadwork, you'd like to see it."

"Yes!" I gasped.

The outer wrapping of the bundle was a piece of hand-woven cotton cloth, once white, but now time-browned and stained. There was a hem along one edge, as if it might have been the hem of a petticoat. Inside the outer cover was a boldly-printed silk bandana—the kind of India silk the traders brought overland from New England to sell to the wealthy southern Indians in the late eighteenth century. When the silk was laid aside, we saw another wrapping, this one of coarse, dark-brown bark cloth, so old that it was beginning to crack and split and shred. Carefully, the chief folded it back, to reveal a wonder—a piece of the fabric the southeastern Indians once wove from the fibres of wild hemp and the down of feathers. It was intact.

"Woodpecker top knots," Chief Dick murmured, his fingers' tips stroking its silkiness.

The feather cloth was the last layer. Inside it were the belts, long strips of purple-blue and blue-white beads. The sinew threads that had been used to weave them into simple, block patterns had dried out and begun to go to pieces. At the bottom of the pile, we saw when the chief had lifted out the belts and laid them aside on the bench, there was a hand-ful of beads that had been released from the rotted strings.

"Seven of them," Chief Dick counted. "One for each of the Cherokee clans. Too bad they're going to pieces. We've got no women who know how to mend them. I wonder if there are any Senecas left who do."

"I think—" I began, and stopped. I snatched a handful of courage, and boldened by the chief's known kindliness, started again. "I think I can mend them—a little," I offered.

Chief Dick smiled richly. "Reckon you could?" he asked.

"I can try," I said. "I may not do very well—not as well as a Seneca could—but I can try."

"We'd be much obliged," he said.

"Wait," I told him. "I've got a mending kit in the car."

It took all afternoon to repair the belts, and the job was not done as well as it should have been then. Each strand should have been loosened, and the beads restrung and re-woven with fresh sinew. But it was done as well as it could be without taking the beads to a laboratory for a month's work, and with the materials that were at hand. I found a spool of white silk buttonhole twist and a fine needle in my kit, and they had to be made to serve our needs.

Sometimes we talked as we sat on the bench in the pool of shade beside the sun-swept clearing, and sometimes we were companionably silent. The chief spoke most often of his grandmother, and remembered things she had told him of the sorrow and shame of the Cherokees on their westward journey. He spoke of the feud, fomented by white men, that had split the tribe before, during, and after the removal, and made this group decide to live in the back of beyond, where only whites who wanted to and had reason would come.

"We've got over hating white people, now," he said once. "Some of them have been mighty good to us. We say they deserve to be Cherokees."

And when Chief Dick and I parted in the level light that shot through the trees to pierce and end the afternoon, he said, "You are a Cherokee now. Come back and dance with us whenever you want to."

I slept again in the room filled with perfumes that night, and drove back to the office the next day. As soon as I reached my desk, I opened Dr. Mooney's volume on the Cherokee. It fell apart to a page ornamented with a drawing of a wampum belt.

"At one time, shortly before the whites landed," Dr. Mooney said, in essence, "the Cherokees and the Senecas are said to have made a lasting peace. Although the tokens have never been identified among the southern tribe, both tribes have legends that agree that the Senecas gave the Cherokees seven wampum belts, one for each clan. It is assumed that the belts were destroyed or lost at the Time of the Trail of Tears—"

CHAPTER 15

BY WAY OF CONTRAST

O NE thing the San Francisco World's Fair of 1939 had that the New York fair of the same year lacked was its Indian exhibition. The government-sponsored display was notable on two counts; as all of us who worked in it were keenly aware. It set a new style in museum technique in the United States, and it brought together Indians from all over the country. There were even, on special occasions, a few from Alaska.

Anyone who labored under the Fenimore-Cooper-engendered notion that all Indians are alike—simply Indians—received a sharply enlightening experience when he attended the San Francisco fair and visited the Indian building. More kinds of Indians were there than I would have dared predict. The potters, basketmakers, silversmiths, spinners and weavers who were present as demonstrators of their skills or as salesmen in the Indian market were housed in Navy barracks on Yerba Buena Island, which was connected with

Treasure Island and the fair by a soaring bridge. From their living quarters on one island the demonstrators and sales-men were daily transported by bus to the Indian building on the other. Each evening after work the Indians returned home in the same way, across the bridge.

The Alaskans, the members of California tribes, and the Chippewa and Winnebago from the Great Lakes states, all of them accustomed to the sight of large bodies of water, paid little attention to the scenery outside the bus windows. The Indians from the southwestern states, on the other hand: the Pima and the Papago, the Apache and the Navaho, and the members of the different Pueblos, were spell-bound and sometimes awe-stricken when they looked around them and saw nothing on either hand but water. Water, to these desert dwellers, was something infinitely precious; each droplet a treasure to be prized as it fell to earth or trickled through the parched trough of an irrigation ditch. Water was not something to be flung about with the lavish osten-tation of an ocean.

Each Indian demonstrator came to San Francisco for a specified length of time, and usually at Indian Service ex-pense. Some of the people remained for two weeks, some for four, and a few, unusually gifted in skills or personality, for a matter of months. If for any reason a demonstrator be-came homesick, no attempt was made to hold him to a previously agreed time. Transportation facilities were im-mediately provided, and he went home at once. A homesick Indian is all too often a dead Indian.

The demonstrators must have gained an amazing assort-ment of impressions of Treasure and Yerba Buena Islands, and of the Bay Area generally. Some, like old Mr. Hands, the Haida totem-pole carver who came from British Columbia, arrived before the fair opened and stayed till just before it

205

closed. All that time Mr. Hands patiently worked his way along a red-wood trunk, perfecting a fifty-foot piece of wood sculpture. He had a pretty clear picture of the City, as well as of the two islands, before he left. Other Indians, who were at the fair for briefer periods of time, went home almost as vague about the geography and customs of the Bay Area as they were when they got off the train.

Each worker was supposed to have one day off each week. Some of them spent their recreation time visiting other displays on Treasure Island; some accepted the invitations of white friends or acquaintances and crossed the Bay to the City to visit; still others, worn out with excitement and the impact of strange, staring eyes, withdrew to the barracks and slept for twenty-four hours.

Serafina Vigil was a pottery demonstrator from one of the New Mexico Pueblos. She was a truly gifted artist. During working hours she was usually surrounded by crowds of visitors. They stood with their eyes riveted to her firmly, surely moving fingers which deftly flowed around the smooth curves of bowls and jars with a certainty of motion that made her downcast, fixed eyes seem unnecessary to the completion of her work. Serafina was perfectly capable of modeling jars blindfolded if she wanted to, but she was as curious about her visitors as they were about her, and she never missed a trick of clothing or gesture among the crowd.

An equally big attraction was Angelina Bellringer, the Navaho weaver. Angelina sat with her back turned to her audience, her fingers crossing and recrossing, working up and then working down again on the patterns of the rug on the loom before her, as secure and practiced as Serafina's flowing hands. It was a little hard on Angelina because she knew the crowds were there beyond the railing at her back, where she could not see them. But rug-weaving, especially when the closer attention must be carried in the artist's head, requires considerably more concentration than does pottery-modeling. There was no question that Angelina's work benefited from her enforced concentration.

In their own surroundings, those two women would probably not have become close friends. Navahos do not mix much with the Indians of the towns, ordinarily. The people of the Pueblos regard the Navahos, their nomadic aggressors since the eleventh century, with awe and some fear. The free-roving Navahos in their turn make no secret of their scorn for the settled, rather plodding farmers, who return from their fields beside the muddy New Mexico streams, each night, to sleep enclosed from all dangers by their house walls.

Nowhere are the differences between the two groups of peoples more clearly shown than in the positions of women in each. The plump, comfortable Pueblo Indian woman is a matriarch, secure in her place as long as she remains among her own people, withdrawn and stricken with shyness when she steps outside the confines of her town. All contacts with the outside world she delegates to her men if she can, and while she may ordain what the men's behavior will be when they leave home, once away from its shelter she will be both placid and tacit in her own conduct. The taller, more rangy Navaho woman, in contrast, appears to be her husband's slave when she is at home, for her work is continuous and his sporadic. But she is an independent, up-standing and down-sitting individual, and the mature Navaho woman is a trader for the average white business man to dread. When she brings a rug or blanket into a trading-post, to exchange for flour or meal or coffee or sugar, she knows in advance exactly what her work is worth in terms of the white man's goods, and woe betide the trader who tries to take advantage of her. Moreover, the Navaho woman is generally a confirmed shopper. Making one purchase at a time, she can string the family grocery order out over two days, in striking contrast to the Pueblo Indian housekeeper, who slides a written list across the counter under the storekeeper's nose, waits for her sack of groceries to be handed to her, and then scuttles home, her shawl wrapped tightly around herself and her bundle.

Both Serafina and Angelina remained at the fair for several weeks. They had brought finished work with them, and their output while they were on Treasure Island was no less than prodigious, especially when one considered the circumstances under which they worked. Under the plan of the exhibition they were allowed to sell their products, and whatever money they received from the sales, less a small percentage paid to the managing Indian cooperative for accommodations, belonged to them. At the end of two months, when the time came for the two women to return to the southwest, each had amassed a considerable sum of money.

We were all sitting in the courtyard, enjoying what we could get of the lemonade-thin San Francisco sun during a rest period, when I noticed that Serafina and Angelina were sitting together, chatting, with apparent ease and amiability, in a mixture of archaic Spanish and government-school-girl English, the contemporary linguae francae of southwestern Indian tribes speaking unrelated languages. Watching the two women, I was delighted to see pleasant and relaxed intertribal relations so well established. Angelina was apparently the dominant personality, as might have been predicted, but Serafina did not seem to object to taking the more minor role. After all, she was away from home and without her husband, who had stayed in New Mexico to cultivate his chile crop.

At the end of the half-hour break I strolled past the two southwesterners, and said hello as I went by. I had no intention of interrupting the women's conversation, although I was consumed by curiosity—professionally-motivated, I hoped—to know what they were talking about. Both returned my greeting amiably, but with a pause after speaking that let me know that there was something they wanted to say to me beyond the formalities. I waited.

"We been thinking—Serafina and me—" Angelina began "—we been wonder, where all the peoples comes from?"

"What people?" I inquired. "People" is a highly flexible word in most Indian languages. It can mean anything from the whole body of mankind to two persons sitting and talking together.

"Peoples who comes to see us. Peoples who watches us work."

"Oh. Well. Some of them come from long ways away—New York and Europe and foreign places like that. And some of them come from Gallup and Winslow and Los Angeles—towns your train went through on the way here. And then a lot of them come from San Francisco, right across on the west side of the Bay."

"What is it—the San Francisco?" That was Serafina, the Indian Catholic. "Is a mission, like at Nambe Pueblo? That church there is the church of the San Francisco like the Cathedral in Santa Fe."

"No," I answered, "not like Nambe, or even Santa Fe. This San Francisco is a city—a big, big town. Bigger than Nambe, than Santa Fe, bigger even than Albuquerque."

It struck me with a somewhat guilty pang that these women had spent the better part of two months within half an hour of the sixth largest city of the nation, and were hardly aware of its existence even after my explanation.

"Is stores in that town?" demanded Angelina, with a gleam in her eyes.

"Big stores," I replied. "All kinds of stores."

"Is stores," repeated Angelina, turning to her Indian friend, and Serafina nodded sedately, as she received this affirmation. Her eyes did not exactly gleam, but they certainly glowed.

The topic was raised again a few days later. This time the weather was overcast and chilly, and we took our rest period on a balcony that overlooked the salesroom. Angelina and Serafina voluntarily joined me, and we gazed out and down at the customers on the floor below us.

"You been that San Francisco?" Angelina began the conversation.

"Oh, yes," I replied. "I go there every night. I live there."

"How you go? Can't walk on water."

"On the ferry boat. It's a big boat that goes back and forth between this island and the city. I come to work every morning and go home every night on that boat."

"Oh." A long pause. Then Serafina asked timidly, "Can anybody ride on that boat? Indians? Or is it just for white peoples?"

"Anybody can ride on it," I said reassuringly, sensing what was coming. "Would you ladies like to ride on the boat to San Francisco?"

There was a breathless pause, prolonging itself almost to the point of unbearability. Then Serafina said briefly, "We like."

Angelina added, "We got lots money. We can pay our own ride."

I laughed. "I'll treat you to the ride," I said. "When would you like to go?"

Again there was unbreathing deliberation of a question. Then,

"We got tomorrow off," Angelina informed me.

Fortunately the hours of government employees at the Indian Exhibition were kept flexible. It was fully understood that time off during the week would be made up for over the weekend; the fair operated on a seven-day week, and someone had to be in the building at all times. We field ethnologists were there as contact persons, and our work consisted as much in keeping the demonstrators happy, their days running smoothly, as explaining to the visitors to the Exhibition the meaning of what they saw. Making my off-day for that week coincide with that of the two Indian women presented no problem.

I crossed to Treasure Island on an early ferry the next morning, and met the demonstrators at the entrance of the exhibition building. They were dressed in their best. I could count the hems of eight ten-yard skirts swinging around Angelina's high-topped red moccasins, and the velveteen blouse under her magenta-chartreuse-and-black-striped shawl was of the most vivid electric blue. Her hands were so loaded with silver and turquoise rings that I wondered how she was able to clutch her purse.

Serafina at first glance appeared to be more modestly attired, for her one-piece wrap-around overdress was of a dark, quiet blue, and it took me a moment to perceive that the hand-spun and hand-woven garment was at least a hundred years old, an heirloom reserved for wear in ceremonial dances when Serafina was at home. Folded around Serafina's shoulders was a magnificent Paisley shawl, of about the same vintage as her dress. Her legs were bound from ankles to knees—at least far above the hem of her dress—in white

211

buckskin bandage-leggings. She wore one ring and one brace-let, both of silver and set with turquoise of almost incredible fineness, the stones precisely matching those dotted through her necklace of white shell beads. My tailored suit and top-coat, while good enough for an ordinary government em-ployee on a shopping trip, were definitely shabby in contrast to the splendor of my companions' garments.

We crossed the island from the government building to the ferry landing on a small motor-train. People on Treasure Island were accustomed to foreigners, from Hindus and Bedouins to Finns and Lapps, in native costumes, so we attracted little attention. Probably not one in a hundred in the hurrying crowds around us could have told what country the Indian women came from; on the other hand, not more than one in fifty, possibly, saw anything outlandish about their wearing what they did, if that were what they wanted to wear. It was all part of the fair.

We went through the barn-like ferry building and along the gangplank to the boat. Angelina sniffed. "Smell funny," she observed.

Serafina glanced around her from beneath her eye-lashes. "Look like barn at Indian school," was her comment.

I was a little surprised. Serafina had not contradicted Angelina, but neither had she uttered her usual tranquil blanket agreement to the other woman's statement. Or-dinarily a Pueblo Indian woman will agree with almost any-body about practically anything in the world to avoid an argument, which even in theory is abhorrent to her.

We went out onto the upper deck, for the day was clear and I wanted these visitors to see, as their first view of San Francisco, the breath-clutching mass of the city climbing the hills around the Bay. Water lapped around the boat as we waited, and both women eyed the oily surface suspiciously.

"Is lots water," Angelina declared.

"Is loooots," Serafina prolonged her agreement. She turned to me. "Why is all in one place?" she queried. "We need water baaad at home; no rain two years and irrigation ditches all dry. Can't government make some way to get part this water to New Mexico?"

"You couldn't use this water for irrigation," I said, intending to be comforting. "This water is all salt."

"Is all salt!" Serafina exclaimed. "Why anybody want all that water if it's no good?"

"Well," I answered, feeling a little at a loss when confronted with this practicality, "ships can travel over it to foreign countries."

"If they don't have all that water," Angelina informed me, "trains can go to foreign countries just as good. Besides, is airplanes can go there anyway. Nobody don't need all this."

There was a sudden whoop from the ferry whistle, and simultaneously the deck of the boat began to tremble under our feet. I sensed that I was alone, and looked around me for my companions. I eventually located them on the lower deck, huddled together in the farthest corner of the ladies' room, as far from the ghastly sound as they could get without jumping overboard. They were still shaken by the beating of the engines as much as by fear. I urged them to come out, but not on any consideration would they return to the haunted exposure of the upper deck. "Is spooks," they informed me in one voice, and their agreement was so complete that I made no attempt to argue with them.

We slid into the slip in San Francisco, mercifully with only a mild snort from the whistle, and as the women felt the trembling of the boat subside they controlled their own. Characteristically, Angelina was first to recover and assert

213

herself. "Is like gov'ment bull, that noise," she said, and laughed shakily.

"Is safe?" Serafina inquired.

"Yes," I reassured them, "it's just wind going through a tube, like a dancer's whistle. It's nothing to be afraid of." My companions listened politely and seemed not in the least convinced by my statement.

I had planned to take these visitors to the city on a ride up Market Street on a trolley car, but I now decided against it. They needed time and a more familiar vehicle in which to recover from the shock of the boat ride. Therefore I piloted them to a taxi, in which they deposited themselves with sighs of relief. Suddenly Serafina sat bolt upright, and stared at me.

"How we going back?" she demanded.

I wondered about that myself. "I'll phone the island when we get to the store," I suggested. "Maybe somebody's coming over with a car this afternoon, and we can drive back with them across the Bridge."

"What if no car?" Angelina questioned.

"Then I guess we'll have to go back on the boat."

"No." Angelina was positive. "If no car, we walk."

I did not protest that the Bridge had no footway. I trusted that I would be able to persuade some fellow-worker to drive over for us. I knew that Angelina was used to walking long distances when she was at home, and that a five mile constitutional, through traffic, across the Bay Bridge, would not daunt her in the least. Rather, my sympathy went out to any driver who had the temerity to get in her way, or to any policeman who might try to argue with her.

The taxi drew up before the store I had selected, and I paid the driver. Angelina was outraged. "He take money for just that little ride?" she wanted to know. "At home peoples

214

gives rides long ways, from Gallup to Prescott, maybe, for nothing."

"Well," I explained lamely, "those are your friends, and I don't know this man. Besides, that's the way he makes his living, taking people for rides where they want to go." As quickly as I could, I switched the subject. "What do you ladies want to buy?" I asked. "Anything special? Or do you want to see what they have in the stores first, and make up your minds about buying later?"

"Stores?" Serafina repeated. "We go to more than one?"

"Yes, we can if you want to. There are lots of stores."

"We go in here first." Angelina took over. Her competence, and her quick recovery from the shock of the boat ride, were equally amazing. "I want store blanket for my old man, shawls for my two little girls, silk shirt for my boy at gov'ment school. If I got money left I buy dress goods for my sisters and my mother. Maybe velvet for blouse for me."

"I want piece goods," Serafina announced. "Maybe pink-and-blue blanket or new sheet for my husband to wear to dances. Is no use to buy groceries, they too heavy to carry on train."

Their program did not sound too ambitious, but I wondered how we could best carry it out. I was afraid to suggest that we ride in an elevator, for there was no way of knowing what its effect would be on the Indians. The only way to reach the piece-goods department seemed to be to climb the stairs. I was sure that would be all right. Both the women saw and climbed stairs daily at Treasure Island.

Inside, the store was not particularly crowded. We had a clear view of the customers at the counters and of the mezzanine above them. Over its railing, at the end facing the door, hung a display of blankets.

"Shawls!" said both women in a single voice, and with

215

united accord they started towards a stairway that rose before them in the direction of the tantalizing spread.

I followed them, watching Angelina move quickly in her full skirts, so she out-distanced Serafina. Serafina was confined by her straight garment and tight leggings. As I pursued them, I saw that the stairway was not immobile. It was an escalator.

Angelina leaped agilely on its lowest tread, and then, while Serafina and I stood rooted to the floor below, we saw her, encompassed in her spreading skirts, soar deliberately upward. We were helpless, Serafina to exclaim, I to attempt explanation or to recover Angelina.

The screams that split Angelina's throat and our eardrums far out-pierced the shrieking of the ferry whistle. Displays trembled on the walls; clerks shuddered behind their counters. And still Angelina soared, and still she screamed.

I passed Serafina in my bound to the rescue, and as I went by her I felt the Pueblo Indian woman seize my hand. Clinging and trembling, but game, she followed me onto the escalator. "She's Navaho," I heard her say beneath her breath, over and over. "She hollered like that. She's Navaho. She hollered." The words seemed to be an incantation and their effect calming, for we stepped off the escalator near the quivering Angelina with Serafina, breathless but comparatively calm.

"It's all right, Angelina," I began, as I pushed my way through the circle of clerks who had gathered around her to see what the matter was. "It's perfectly all right—"

"It went," Angelina quavered. "I step on them stairs and they went—" Her voice died away in Athabascan sobs which neither Serafina nor I could comprehend.

"It's all right—" I repeated helplessly, this time to the salesladies, motioning them away from us. Still bewildered,

216

they withdrew to their stations, leaving us more or less alone. I turned to Serafina. Perhaps if Angelina saw and heard me soothing her friend, it would have a comforting effect on her. "We're all safe, Serafina," I commenced, and stopped.

"She's hollered. She's Navaho and she's hollered," Serafina ended her incantation. "You and me went up them walking stairs and we didn't holler. Navahos is 'fraid of things too."

I nodded, for all words had left me. Common humanity had closed my mind to comparisons of tribal characteristics, and I was amazed that Serafina should be so concerned with the problem.

"All my life they tells me, 'Navaho womens 'fraid of nothing!' " Serafina announced. "All my life I hears peoples say Pueblos got to respect Navahos, 'cause Navahos don't gets scare."

I continued to nod, feeling that the habit was growing on me and would soon be uncontrollable.

"My husban' go shopping for us at home," Serafina reflected aloud. "Angelina, she use' to do her own shopping. She go stores, go trading-posts, she buy what she want. I never done that." She deliberated only briefly. Then she took hold of Angelina's arm and shook her, firmly, as she might a recalcitrant child. "Come on," Serafina commanded. "What you cryin' 'bout? You want go buy blankets at stores, don't you? Well, here is store, there is blankets, you still got your purse. Come on, we goin' shoppin'. I buy checked blanket, and you buy blanket with stripes."

CHAPTER 16

THE END OF A BEAUTIFUL FRIENDSHIP

Todas Cosas—which name means Everything—came from that section of Arizona that looks like Inner Mongolia. The red rocks wall in the green canyons, and the colors are no more sharply in contrast than are those chosen by the Navahos of that remote world for their clothing.

Todas Cosas was tall and lean and white-haired. His cheek bones were high and jutting, and they were framed by side locks that straggled from beneath the red bandana bound around his forehead. He was a medicine man and his Power forebade him to wear shoes, so he went always with his levis tucked into the tops of red-dyed buckskin legging-moccasins. Use of the Power had brought Todas Cosas rewards in the form of all sky blue turquoise chunks to hang from his long ear-lobes, and a silver necklace from which swung a crescent of silver studded with more clear blue stones. He wore rings and bracelets of silver, and the stones mounted in them were the finest that were to be had.

Like all medicine men, Todas Cosas was extremely intelligent. His philosophy could be summed up, "If you can't lick 'em, jine 'em." He made friends with the Indian Service administrators in key positions—the same men the Washington office looked upon with approval. Todas Cosas' reasoning in the matter of political friendships was entirely direct. These were the men who controlled the lives of The People —as the Navaho speak of themselves. If a man knew what these men thought and planned, that man would be in a position to talk more helpfully to his People. And helping his People was his life's work.

The administrators recognized that Todas Cosas was a power in the land and a personality in his own right. He was no more anxious to hold and use their friendship than they were to hold and use his. It all made for fine public relations, and both sides benefited thereby.

In time the Indian Service Superintendent invited Todas Cosas to come to his office, to sit down, and to smoke. And when these formalities had been duly observed, the Superintendent read to the old man from a paper that was before him on his desk. Todas Cosas' nephew translated the words of the letter. There was an Indian Fair to be held at San Francisco. The leading men of many tribes were invited to attend. They would be given food and a place to stay and so much money—cash—for every day that they were away from their homes. In return, they would be asked to demonstrate their skills. Todas Cosas was known as a painter in sands— one who made the pictures that were part of the healing ceremonies. Would he go to San Francisco and show the white people, who were ignorant of such matters, how sand paintings were made?

Todas Cosas gave the matter the deliberation it deserved. At the end of half-an-hour's thought, he inquired, "Are all

219

the white people who come to the fair ignorant of sand paintings?"

"Tell him," said the Superintendent, "that they are. They can't help being."

"All of them? Every one? Surely some of them must have been on this reservation at some time. If they came here, they could have seen sand paintings."

"The men in charge of the Indian Fair have been here. They have seen sand paintings made."

Again Todas Cosas deliberated, and at the end of a second half hour he spoke again.

"He says," the nephew reported after listening attentively, "that you know a sand painting is part of a healing ceremony. It must be made between the rising and the setting of the sun, and it must be wiped out and rubbed on the sick person's body at sundown. Will the sick people of San Francisco come to him for healing? He can treat only four of them in one month. There are perhaps other medicine men who can treat more, and he knows some who can treat only four in a year."

This presented a serious problem. The Superintendent considered matters in his turn.

"Has he ever made a sand painting just to show someone how it was made?" he asked at last.

There was a long discussion. "He never made a real one," the nephew announced at length. "When he was a young man and just learning, he filled in the plain parts of the sand paintings for the man who taught him. Now he's teaching me and I do that part of the work for him, and he makes the design parts—the interesting ones. But he says that one time, years ago, at the Indian Fair in Gallup, he made an imitation sand painting to show the white people there how it was done. He worked on it, a little at a time, for four days, and he made mistakes as he went along. If it had been right, and had been a real sand painting, it would have killed him if he took four days to make it."

"Well, he seems to have survived."

"Oh, doing it that way didn't make him sick, even. That's because he made the mistakes. He says he could do that in San Francisco. He could take his time and make lots of mistakes, and it would be all right. But he says you have to let those white men who understand about sand paintings know in advance what he's going to do, so they won't think he's lying or ignorant."

"I can do that. I'll write them a letter today."

"And he says I have to go with him, and get my room and meals and half as much money as he does, so he can have a helper to fill in the backgrounds."

"That can be arranged. You plan on going too. Does he want to take his wife?"

"He says, which one?"

The Superintendent shook his head. "Tell him I didn't hear what he said." All the men laughed when this was translated, and the atmosphere of the room became more relaxed.

"He sure is particular," the nephew observed as the old man got to his feet. "He's got all sorts of rules. Can't have anyone that eats fish near him—all kinds of things."

"Nobody who eats fish?"

"That's what he says. Those old people, you know, they believe fishes are their ancestors. They think anybody who eats fish is a cannibal."

The Superintendent jotted a note on the margin of the letter on his desk. When he answered it later in the day, he added to his other information, "If possible, I believe it would be advisable not to allow fish to be served in Todas

221

Cosas' presence. I realize that some of the Indians in the group are Catholics, and I hope the problem will not be too complicated to solve. Perhaps if Todas Cosas can be given his day off on Friday, so that he need not see the fish served and eaten—"

Old Mr. Hands was a Haida from British Columbia. He had learned to work in wood almost as soon as he could walk—certainly from the time he could be shown how to hold a jackknife point down. Wood was his love and work in wood his art. When Mr. Hands came to San Francisco, bringing his son with him to do the crude preliminary hacking and carving that cannot be expected of a great artist, he also brought with him on the freighter a fifty foot redwood trunk. Mr. Hands, aged eighty, was known the length of the Pacific Coast as the finest carver of totem poles the Haida had ever produced.

The totem-pole-to-be was too long, and took up too much space, to go in the steam-heated area that sheltered the other Indian demonstrators. Instead, it had to be laid horizontal, supported on trestles, in the courtyard outside the space. San Francisco summers are not noted for their warmth, for they bear a strong resemblance to winters in other parts of the country. Fortunately, Mr. Hands did not care. Winters in British Columbia were more severe than anything a San Francisco summer could provide, and he was used to working outdoors in January. He made sure the bole of the tree was right side up, and, whistling a mournful Haida song under his breath, produced a majestic set of eighteenth century Russian shipwright's tools, inherited from his great grandfather, and, as well as anyone not Haida could discern, went cheerily to work. The Haida are not famed for the lightness of their spirits on any occasion.

At that time my own work at the Indian market was concentrated on beadworkers from the Plains tribes. Most of them were elderly women. They had come to the fair fully equipped with the tools of their trade: rawhide, soft-tanned buckskin, beads, and sinew. They formed a cohesive group, for although they were drawn from several tribes their backgrounds were similar and they were about of an age. Each morning when they arrived at the workroom there was a slight, busy stir, and then they subsided into stitching, stringing beads, trading materials and ideas, and talking in English of their grandchildren, cookery, and operations. The atmosphere surrounding the beadworkers was delightfully homey, scented as it was with the faint minty puffs of their sweetgrass sachets and the stronger musk of smoke-tanned hides. It was a charming section of the workroom to linger in, but one where lingering was on my part pure self-indulgence. If ever any group of women was entirely, blissfully self-contained, that one was.

So, when I had said good morning and chatted for a few minutes with Mrs. Luke Big Turnip and Mrs. James White Man, I was to some extent at a loose end. I had to be on call, in case of desperate emergencies in the sinew department (sinew does not take kindly to damp climates and requires slow periodic drying over electric hot plates), but otherwise I had time on my hands. I took to going out into the courtyard to watch old Mr. Hands at work.

Some old men you can call Uncle Jim, and some you may even call Jimmy, but nobody ever called old Mr. Hands anything but old Mr. Hands, as far as I know. He was not intentionally forbidding, but he was a good deal older than anybody else around the exhibition, and he certainly stood on his dignity. However, he was perfectly willing to talk, and he could talk and work simultaneously. I learned all I know

about Haida woodcarving from old Mr. Hands on those
foggy San Francisco mornings, when the ferries moaned up
and down the Bay.

Mr. Hands, as might have been expected, was carving his
family tree on the redwood trunk. He told me—he spoke fair
English—that he had always meant to do it, but he had
been so busy working in the shipyards in Vancouver or carving totems for other people in his spare time that this was
his first opportunity to work on his own crest. Naturally
enough, he said, he would not take the pole back home
with him. In the first place, he lived right in town, and even
if the municipal authorities encouraged the erection of
totem poles in residential districts, there was no place to put
one without taking up the sidewalk. In the second place,
since he was being paid for the time he spent in working, and
the government had paid the freight on the pole to San Francisco, the pole belonged to the United States Department
of the Interior. He had asked if there were any special design
he should carve for the government, and when he was told
there was not, he had allowed himself the indulgence of
finally making his own family tree.

The back of the trunk had been scooped out before ship-
ping, to make the pole lighter. This cut down freight charges
and made the wood easier for the carvers to handle. Mr.
Hands would indicate on the trunk the area to be roughed
out, and his son would hack away, showering the ground
around them with biggish chips. As soon as the form was
roughed, the father would take over and begin to execute the
finished shapes, and the delicate details of the carving. Ultimately, the entire totem pole was to be brightly painted with
barn paint. The thought of that saddened me, for it seemed
a shame to conceal the beautiful grain of the wood and the
incredible fineness of the feathering surface with anything,

but I was a minority of one. Both the Hands looked forward cheerily to the day when they could take up their brushes and splash.

They started at the base of the pole and worked up, and as they went they left behind them the blocky forms of mythological creatures.

"What's that one?" I inquired when the first was finished.

"That man the bear," said old Mr. Hands.

"And what's that you're working on now?"

"That man the eagle."

"What comes next?"

"I don' know."

The son turned his head, without raising it, to speak to me.

"He ain't allowed to tell till it takes shape," he explained.

I nodded and subsided. After that, I kept my questions to myself and waited for explanations until people were ready to give them. I was curious as to what the final outcome would be, but not impatiently so. Maybe there would be a whale, or a sculpin—.

From time to time it occurred to me that perhaps Mr. Hands was lonely. Maybe he would like somebody of his own age and sex to talk to. The beadworkers were united against the world: Cheyenne, Sioux, Comanche, and Blackfoot, they were amiably cohesive. The makers of pottery, whatever the relations of their Pueblos when they were at home, were at peace and at one now they were away. The silversmiths and the weavers were as united, and basket-makers from all over the country swapped ideas and materials as cheerfully as the beadworkers did. It was all lovely and warm and cordial. Only poor old Mr. Hands was left out. There were no other older men—all the silversmiths were young sprouts recently out of government schools. There

225

were no other woodcarvers, except his son, and his son was courting a waitress in the Japanese pavilion and was away from his father except during business hours. No, I thought, Mr. Hands must surely be lonesome and bored. I hoped he wouldn't want to go home before he finished the totem pole on that account.

Then I heard that the sand painter was coming, and that he was an old man. We had waited and hoped for a sand painter—a really good one, through whose fingers the colored sands would flow on the flat earthen floor with deft certainty—ever since the fair opened. Our aspirations had never risen much above a youngster, probably an apprentice who would lack the surety of a master. We were all overwhelmed with excited delighted flattery when we learned that no less a personality than Todas Cosas was coming among us. We had all known of him before.

Todas Cosas and his nephew got into San Francisco on the evening train. They were met by an official delegation, of which I was not a member. Only our biggest official guns were included. I stayed home like a good girl and saw that the beadworkers were back in their quarters and settled to the interminable basket-dice game that occupied their evenings.

On the following morning, while I was wondering how to arrange a meeting between old Mr. Hands and Todas Cosas, the bus pulled into the courtyard and the two old men got out. I was spared deciding whether to take the woodcarver to the sand painter or vice versa, for not only did they leave the bus together, it was clear that they had already established their means of communication. Mr. Hands started purposefully for his totem pole, and Todas Cosas came right along with him. Together they inspected the carvings of the bear and the eagle. Todas Cosas approved of the eagle, that was

226

plain, but he hung fire over the bear. At last he addressed his nephew, who had trailed along behind the two older men with the younger Mr. Hands.

The nephew in turn spoke to the son, who explained that the pole was a record of his father's family, and that the bear was included because of an ancestress who had belonged to the bear clan.

"Bears is out, for us," said the younger Navaho. "We don't go near 'em, or even talk about 'em. How far back was this old bear lady?"

Young Hands consulted his father. They both counted on their fingers. "She's five grandfathers back of him," Hands reported. "That's why she's at the bottom."

Todas Cosas' nephew nodded his head, back and then forward, and interpreted the explanation. The old man held up five fingers, and everybody counted them. Apparently five was a safe number, for they all grinned and nodded cheerfully, and the sand painters went off to the place that had been assigned to them, an area intended to suggest the interior of a hogan, in which a healing ceremony would properly take place.

From that day on it was apparent that my concern about a friend for Mr. Hands could end. Except on their days off, the two old men were inseparable most of the time outside working hours. They smoked and talked endlessly, at first using the younger sand painter or one of the silversmiths or even a woman weaver as an interpreter; later communicating directly with one another by some means they devised for themselves.

Mr. Hands' day off was Wednesday, and on Wednesdays he repaired by ferry to Fisherman's Wharf. He was engaged in eating his way from one end of it to the other, trying a different fish dish at a different stall each week. Neither

227

boats nor the denizens of the deep held any terrors for him; he had lived with and on both his entire life. He boggled neither at raw oysters nor fried squid, but happily conducted his one-man cook's tour of the most famous fish-serving area in a fish-eating city.

Todas Cosas' day off was scheduled, as the Superintendent had suggested, for Friday. On that day, someone on the staff saw to it that he and his nephew were away from the island from breakfast—since they were ritually forbidden to eat eggs, they invariably breakfasted on shredded wheat, oatmeal, and cream of wheat before going to work—until well after dinner time. Not all the other Indians ate fish, but none was so tabu-bound as the Navahos. They did not feel that they were witnessing acts of cannibalism if they watched other people consume fish.

Finding all-day occupations for two Navahos in San Francisco was not the easiest thing in the world, and sometimes it required careful planning. They could, and did, spend some time at the fair itself, visiting the other exhibits. They were entranced with the biological one, in which plaster models of embryos, in different stages of development, were shown. The nephew explained that they had known that sheep and horses and deer grew in that way, and had surmised it to be true of human beings, but this was their first definite confirmation of the fact. On the other hand, they were not enthusiastic about the Fine Arts display, and asked as tactfully as possible if white people really *liked* to look at ugly things? The source of this question proved to be a little gem of an O'Keefe composition, focused on a horse scapula.

Away from the island, the Navahos visited the zoo, the palace of fine arts in the city, Chinatown, and the other tourist sights of San Francisco. Todas Cosas was profession-

228

ally interested in the Cathedral, and spent most of a day examining it. He was not interested in the hospitals. They were almost exactly like the hospital back at Ganado—and he had never been entirely convinced that hospitals were constructed for any other reason than to shelter the dying, safely away from their families, so that hogans would not have to be torn down and the living put to the trouble of moving.

So the weeks passed. Todas Cosas and his nephew executed sand painting after sand painting—all wrong, of course, but as beautiful to white eyes as if they had been right. Mr. Hands worked his way steadily along his redwood trunk. From time to time each of the old men took a few minutes to examine the other's work. They were impressed with one another's skill, and it was evident that they formed a mutual admiration society. Todas Cosas even made a sand painting that was right from start to finish—on a Sunday—to cure Mr. Hands' rheumatism, and he was greatly taken with the raven, the beaver, and the sea otter as they took their places along the pole.

The end of the fair was approaching. Summer had given way to fall, and the weather at last was bright and sunny. Mr. Hands had many more visitors than he had earlier in the season, and most of us sat around in the thin sunlight that filled the courtyard to eat our lunch. The upper end of the pole had been reached, and the space occupied by the final figures grew smaller as the diameter of the pole decreased. We could see the work progress from day to day now. It could have been that Mr. Hands was hurrying a little in order to get to his paint splashing before it was time to go home.

On a Thursday he started to carve the last figure, and by noon it was well along. Todas Cosas was late coming out for lunch, and he sat down to eat his sandwich before he did

229

anything else. Then seeing that his friend also had finished eating, he strolled over to speak to him and to take a look at the totem pole.

It was a long, unhappy look, and the face that Todas Cosas raised to us at its end was a bitter one. For the topmost figure, the one that represented our Mr. Hands himself, was indeed a sculpin, a fish that was carved with the most loving attention to detail. Todas Cosas summoned his nephew with a jerk of his head and an inclusive sweep of his arm. Young Hands, sensing trouble, also came up on a run.

"Ask him who that is," Todas Cosas commanded. The nephew complied.

"That man me," Mr. Hands answered, puzzled but amiable.

"He's a fish."

"Sure I'm a fish. That man there, that's me. He's my name."

"The old man says that is bad luck; the worst luck. Only thing could be worse would be to eat fish."

"Sure I eat fish," Mr. Hands said without hesitation. "All kinds of fish. If he can get off on Wednesday—that's my day —I take him down to the wharf. He can eat fish there he never tasted before; never even heard of."

Todas Cosas did not wait for the invitation to be translated. As soon as he heard the affirmative he straightened, and wrapped his striped blanket around him. "Chindi! (Ghost!)" he said in the most scathing of Navaho denunciations. Trailed by his nephew he marched into the office and demanded his time, and immediate transportation back to Arizona, away from this country of cannibals. There was no holding him, and that night, on the train from Oakland, home he and his nephew went.

Mr. Hands watched his friend vanish into the office, bewildered. His face looked like that of an aged child that has lost its ice cream cone. He finished his carving that day and slapped the paint on it the next, without bothering to take time off. On Thursday night he left on the boat for Vancouver.

CHAPTER 17

THE AUTOGRAPHING

Iₙ a previous chapter of this book, I have indicated that the Indian Arts and Crafts Board suspended operations during the war years. My personal war job was with the American Red Cross, because I was free to travel and knew something about the southwestern states and their peoples. I have never known whether I actually accomplished anything during those years; I was too busy at the time and too utterly tired afterwards to be capable of appraisal.

Only one thought persisted when I was on the edge of sleep and thoughts about anything but the day's problems passed over my mind. I wanted, with a desperate homesickness, to get back to research. So, at the war's end, I secured a fellowship and retired to a quiet corner of New Mexico to work. A friend joined me for a visit, and we decided to spend a winter in the sun. I would do research and nothing but research. She would paint landscapes. In the intervals, we planned to rest.

The worst thing about being habitually active is that the habit persists. We threw ourselves into our work ten hours a day and into housekeeping and repairing the rest of the time. The roof over our heads had become our hobby, we said blithely.

I had chosen to work in a Pueblo because I knew little about the Indians of the towns at first hand. I wanted to do a real research problem, not simply to pour old wine into new bottles. The Plains drew me; I knew and loved the people there. But I knew the fundamentals of Plains Indian life thoroughly, and Elizabeth had sometimes said, as a joke, that I was more Indian than any of her tribe. If that were true, I thought I should be able to transfer my feeling and understanding to another group of people. The Indians of the Pueblos were as different from those of the Plains as any people of the same blood could possibly be. So my choice fell on the towns of the Rio Grande.

There was another reason. Back in 1939, in what looked from 1945 like another world, and one that now could never be recaptured, Maria Martinez and her husband, Julian, had come to the San Francisco fair to demonstrate their methods of pottery making. I had known them both slightly there, and had liked and admired them. Now Julian was dead and Maria was aging. It was time—high time—that a record was made of their life and work. With Maria's consent, I undertook the making of that record.

The task was not easy, nor had I expected it to be. For days on end Maria and I sat and faced one another across her living room. When the work first began, it was with the understanding that she could talk to me only about the things that had happened to her. The council of her Pueblo forbade us to discuss anything concerned with the religion or the government of Maria's town. At first I tried asking questions, but I soon discovered that it was impossible for me to frame them so that they did not impinge on the forbidden topics.

At last I drew a deep breath, and plunged into the stream-of-consciousness method of interviewing. I had used it before, but only with persons I knew well. Maria and I were still comparative strangers to one another. But I ventured the suggestion that she choose the subject on which we would talk each day. If anything were not clear to me, then I would have to ask questions necessary for understanding the point, but I promised that they should be as few as possible.

The work went better after that agreement had been reached. Maria talked more readily, and she relaxed more completely, when she felt that she was in control of an interview. For weeks and months she talked and I wrote. Then the day came when she said, gently, "I think that's all I have to tell you." I went home to the other side of the valley to put my field notes in order and to coax from them a coherent story of one woman's life.

Nothing in the world can be more still than a Pueblo on an ordinary day. On a feast day, when a ceremonial dance is publicly performed, there is movement and life in the village, and voices speak and laugh, always softly. Visiting a Pueblo on a feast day is exciting, for you bring away from it then a feeling of liveliness.

But on a regular weekday there is nothing to break the calm of the rows of adobe houses and the stillness that envelopes them. Perhaps, in the early morning or late afternoon, children and dogs may play briefly in the plaza. But from the hour when school opens until the time when it closes, there is a minimum of sound and movement. The Indians of the towns are busy people. The men are occupied in the fields or along the irrigation ditches, and the women are absorbed and consumed by their houses and their pottery making.

This stillness, so unlike the continual coming and going about a Plains Indian home, frightened me at first. I thought there must be illness—even death—in the closed, silent houses. Then, as I became more familiar with the place and more accustomed to its ways, I perceived that the quiet was an integral part of the life pattern of these Indians. All their being was encompassed by the group, as it was inclosed by their houses and as the houses formed a wall about the town. Impossible that the silence, or the sheltering wall, should give way to admit the noise and clutter of individualism. People spoke always of "our houses" and "our ways." No one would have claimed individual ownership of either.

Yet Maria, the individual, had been outside the wall. She had traveled from coast to coast, showing and teaching strangers how her pottery was made. She was famous; museums in foreign countries collected her jars and bowls. Almost everyone who came to New Mexico knew her name, and most of the travelers visited her home. Her guest book was a record of the great and near great who had come and gone in the southwest for twenty years or more. She had been interviewed and photographed and painted and sculped. Maria Martinez—the woman—was famous.

Fame did not make her happy. She did not like being, even a little, different from the other women of her town. She spent much time teaching the younger women how to make pottery, and helping them to sell it. Maria said to me once that she wished visitors to the Pueblo would look more closely at the work of the other potters, for many of them were more skilled than she. Maria was honest and realistic about her own ability. She knew how to do her work, but so did many other women.

I have never been sure that fame made Maria unhappy, however. She accepted it and she lived with it; she did not avoid visitors, and she never refused requests to pose for photographs, even holding babies. Many tourists interrupted our work, several for hours-long intervals. I grew impatient and ruffled of temper; Maria never did.

We were friends. We could not have worked together had we not been. All the same, we were formal friends. Maria called me by my given name, as was the right of an older woman speaking to a younger one. I never called her, and never in my wildest dreams thought of her, as anything but "Mrs. Martinez." I had the deepest respect for her, as an artist and as a woman, a respect that increased as time passed and I knew her better and better.

But I was never sure how she felt about me, except that I knew she was friendly. That was evident. It was also evident, presently, that a book as a book had little meaning for her. She could not comprehend exactly what went into the making of it. She asked me once how many books there would be when I finished—would there be enough for her sons to have one apiece. I explained that there would probably be five thousand copies.

"All just alike?"

"All exactly alike."

She looked at my fingers, clutched around my pencil. "How will you do it? How long will it take you?"

Suddenly I saw that she was thinking of books in terms of jars and bowls, each made separately by the same pair of hands. I tried to explain about printing and binding. I am not sure that she understood me, or, if she did, whether she believed me.

The manuscript was finished at last, and almost to the day that I completed it the publisher wrote my friend

Martha, asking her to illustrate the book. Martha undertook the assignment reluctantly. She was not an illustrator; she was a landscape artist and a portraitist. But the thought of having the book illustrated with photographs was more than she could bear, once she saw my attempts at photography. She agreed to make a set of line drawings and of studies of Maria's pottery. She decided that she would try a portrait of Maria, in line, to be used as a frontispiece.

We went to the Pueblo, and I explained the plan to Maria. She agreed to it. As we were about to leave, she asked me,

"What does it say in the book?"

Her question startled me. I was about to send the manuscript away for final processing, and she did not know what it contained. For all I knew, it might contain a great deal of matter that was offensive to her.

"Would you like to read it?" I asked.

Maria debated with herself a moment. "*You* read it," she said finally.

When the sitting began the next day, it was to the accompaniment of my reading of the manuscript. Maria sat on a small stool before us, her head bowed, her hands clasped loosely in her lap, and listened. Her pose was one of utter, controlled calm, and Martha furnished a little, under-breath, whistling obligato of sheer pleasure in her model as the reading went on. After an hour, we heard a door close somewhere in the rear of the house, and Maria shifted infinitesimally. Martha looked at her watch.

"Oh," she exclaimed, "you must be tired! Don't you want to move around and rest a little?"

"Yes," said Maria composedly. She rose with only the slightest stiffness and left the room. In fifteen minutes she was back, smiling.

"My son," she explained. "His first gran'baby was born

237

last night. He just got back from the hospital to tell me. It's a girl."

"You're a great-grandmother now?" we asked in an excited duet.

"First time," said Maria composedly, resuming the pose. Her facial expression had altered to an almost smile, and so the frontispiece shows her, a little like an Indian Mona Lisa.

There was only one serious interruption to the reading after that. At a certain point in the story of her life, Maria raised her hand to stop me.

"How did you know about that?" she queried. "I know I never told you."

"I knew you," I answered. "I know what you would do if certain things happened to you."

"It happened." She waited a moment. "But it wasn't my father who gave me good advice about marriage and my duties. The man who told me those things was the religious leader of our town." I made the necessary correction and we went on, without her asking for another change anywhere in the book.

There followed the usual delay that precedes the publication of any book. You have time to be relieved and happy about finishing it, regretful for omissions, sleepless about inaccuracies that *must* have slipped by you somehow, and finally absorbed in new work and forgetful of what is past.

At last came the letter announcing the publication day. Soon afterwards came another, from a bookstore, suggesting an autographing party, to launch the volume. "We look forward to having the writer and the illustrator with us," wrote the owner of the bookstore, "and we hope, too, that it will be possible for you to persuade Maria Martinez to come to the party. We are sure people will like to meet the subject of the book, and secure her autograph with the others."

I was indignant at the suggestion, for I was convinced that Maria had had enough of being a monkey on a stick to last more than a lifetime. But I dutifully relayed the invitation to her.

"You going?" she asked. I nodded.

"And Martha?"

"Yes, Martha is going with me."

"We be back that night?"

"Yes, if you want to be. Otherwise we can stay at a hotel."

"I come home."

"All right. We'll all come home."

I marked the date of the party on the calendar, and reported to Martha.

"What do you suppose she'll wear?" the illustrator inquired.

I shook my head. We had never seen Maria in anything but the type of dresses worn by the older women of the Pueblo, patterned after the ones their ancestresses had worn for a thousand years. We both hoped that Maria would stick to her own wardrobe, and not experiment with white woman's dress.

We should have trusted her. Her dress was of printed silk, with a background of plum color, and it was made in the old style. Her jewelry, of silver and turquoise, was magnificent and looked too heavy for one woman to wear. When the bookstore owner pinned a bouquet of jonquils on her shoulder, she glowed with delight at the final touch of magnificence.

We sat down at the table provided for us. All about us were heaped new, clean copies of the book, shiny and redolent of printers' ink. Maria considered them.

"Where we sign?" she asked.

"Here," said Martha. She opened a book to the frontispiece, and showed Maria where to write her name, just under
the drawing. Maria took the pen, and composedly signed
the portrait as she would have a finished pot. Later we
received complaints from purchasers who thought her fine
caligraphy was part of the reproduction, and we had to display mint copies to convince them that it was genuine.

The publisher had sent a representative to attend the
autograph party. She, as well as each of us, received a bouquet, but none of the three was quite as big or beautiful as
Maria's.

Autographing parties are wearing concerns. For me they
are divided sharply, into the periods when I am in terror
that nobody will come and the periods when I wish they
would all go home. Meantime I smile and smile and scribble
my name, and straighten my cramped fingers and do it again.
My face aches, my fingers ache, my back aches, and I want
nothing in the world but a cup of tea and a hot footbath.

But Maria took it all in her stride. She did not smile in
a stiff, face-cracking grimace. She grinned cordially at one
and all, and she meant it. I sat at one end of the table and
she at the other, with Martha between us. And to everyone
who greeted her, "Remember me, Maria? I was at your home
and bought a bowl two years ago?" she gave a heart-warming
smile and a polite "Yes," which could have been an answer
to the question or an assent to the purchase.

When it was all over, and we had had the longed-for cup
of tea, followed by dinner, we got in the car and started home
with Martha at the wheel.

"I don't see how you do it," the publisher's representative
said to her once. "I know you're dead on your feet, and this

road would be hard to drive if you were fresh, but you keep right on going."

"Martha does everything good," said Maria in the darkness. In her voice was the pride that one good craftsman shows for the accomplishments of another. I understood its source. She and Martha had the gift of the hands in common. They were one. I could not join them.

Maria did not speak again until we stopped before her home. For all I know, she slept the whole way back to the Pueblo. Then, with the car still, she roused herself to step out into the night. A light burned in a window of the house —the only light in the totally dark and silent village.

"Good night," Maria said to us. "The boys is waiting up to hear what people said 'bout my book what Alice wrote down." A shaft of light received her into the open door and she vanished from us. I sank limply back into my corner of the car. I, too, was justified.

CHAPTER 18

THE TOP OF THE MESA

By the time Martha and I had lived in New Mexico for three years, I had become accustomed to a world that was bounded by mountains. I had never lived day after day with mountains before, so I cannot say whether the way I responded to them was a usual one.

At first I loved the mountains extravagantly and foolishly, as I might love the fine binding of a new book or the taste of a new and strange and delicious food. Then there came a period in which I was indifferent to the mountains. During this time they enclosed my physical horizon without my being aware of either horizon or enclosure. Then I entered on what promised to be my final mood, one of warm liking and affection, of tolerance and exchange of strength. This last must be rather like the mood of a good and lasting marriage, from what my friends tell me.

Still, as in any marriage, sharp little annoyances sometimes jar my relationship with the mountains. Smooth, rounded shoulders and abrupt peaks I can accept; they have

242

been a part of any normal and well-behaved mountain of which I ever heard. But what is there to say or do about a mesa that projects itself into the valley at the foot of the main slope? That is no place for a mesa. A proper mesa is out on a plain, where its form and bulk can mean something. Here it was, dwarfed by the slopes above it, and engulfed by the surrounding floor of the valley.

That little mesa began to annoy me seriously after a time. It was not aggressive; it was a calm sort of mesa; certainly it did not go out of its way to get on my nerves. But it was *there*; outside the window when I looked up from my work; beyond the patio when I glanced away from pouring tea; rising well within view of the gate when I drove home at night. I was constantly reminded of that mesa; I never had a chance to forget it.

The mesa did nothing at all. The mountains sent water and rocks and sometimes up-rooted trees crashing down into the valley. Thunder heads gathered above the mountains, and sound rumbled down onto the houses below. The mesa never indulged in pyrotechnics. All of it stayed right where it was. Long ago everything that could roll had coursed down the mesa's steep straight sides. Its top was too low for a gathering place for clouds. The mesa stayed at home and minded its own business. There was no discernible reason why I should not do likewise.

Consciously, I never thought of climbing the mesa and so discovering something about its character. To know and understand anything is to become tolerant and gentle towards it, as much with a mesa as with a human being. I had walked all my life on the level earth of the plains, the thought of walking straight up in the air did not occur to me. The mesa and I were a respectful distance apart. One seemed as likely as the other to make the first approach.

243

An old Indian woman first suggested to me the possibility of climbing. She was telling me stories; the small folktales that her people told to children. "That happened long times ago," she said, casually. "They say in those ole days people live on top of the li'l mesa."

"What do you call the mesa?" I asked, recording place names automatically.

"We call it The Mesa Where the Deer Leaped Down," said Concepción. She smiled reminiscently. "There's a canyon on the north side of the mesa," she explained. "It's narrow and steep, with a track along it. When we were children my sister and I use' to go 'long the canyon till we were 'bout half ways up. It's like a ladder there. You can see deer's tracks on the ground."

"What is on top of the mesa?" I demanded.

"That I don't know of myself," Concepción replied. "They use' to tell us when we were children that the li'l people of the earth live' there. Las' spring school teacher took the children up, and my li'l grandsons went all the ways to the top. They said there use' to be a pueblo there, but the people all gone any more."

The idea took possession of me. Here was a chance to find out something about the personality of the small, persistent mesa. I thought about the climb, and I suppose I must have talked about it, for a week later Martha said to me,

"Why don't we take Concepción and the children, and go and climb the thing?"

"Take lunch and have a picnic?" I hazarded.

"Yes, if you want to," Martha assented. "It isn't far, and the children will probably enjoy it."

I mentioned the matter to Concepción that afternoon.

"Yes," she said. "Why not? Let's do it soon. Now is the

244

warm time of the year, in October. Now leaves turning and things is pretty. We go on Sunday. The children and I be ready."

They were all ready on Sunday, three little boys and an old lady, waiting outside her house in the Pueblo, with gunny-sack bundles under their arms and shyly expectant smiles on their faces. They all climbed into the back seat of the car, and Concepción announced,

"You follow the road to the east out of the Pueblo, and after while it fork. Then I tell you which road to take."

I drove slowly for the road was rough and the car jolted over it, and soon we traveled along what was little more than a trail. The little boys in the back seat twittered in their own language like excited birds, and Concepción hushed them sometimes, competently. Martha and I, in the front seat, did not speak at all. Perfect concentration was required of both of us if the road were to be followed.

At the fork, one track led off through the low pine trees and junipers, going upward toward the mountain slopes where the high timber grew. The other trail dipped lower, curving suddenly into a patch of russet elm and golden cottonwood. There was a metallic flash of water running quickly and smoothly through the trees, and Concepción said,

"That the river there. I guess if people ever live on top the mesa, they must got their water there."

I was surprised by the approach to the mesa side. From a distance the hill had seemed to rise sheer from the valley floor, and I had not expected to find trees and a river at its foot.

"People lived here, Grandma," one of the children said. "We saw the place where they lived, and the pieces of their bean pots."

"They say it was a pueblo here," Concepción repeated what she had said before. "My grandma always say it was the li'l people of the earth that live here, no Indians, but school teacher tole these children it was jus' an old pueblo."

"What became of the little people of the earth?" I asked.

And Concepción replied, "They wen' underground when human people began to get too strong and mean. Nobody ever see them any more."

I parked the car under the shade of a big, twisted cotton-wood and we left it there unlocked, with our lunch and cooking untensils lying open for the world to see. The world that saw was a herd of half a dozen half-wild horses, who peered at us and fled through the undergrowth. Why lock the car, when the horses would not like our lunches if they tried to eat them?

A tree had fallen across the stream, and we trod on this bridge, with the water running steadily and gently and strongly below us. On the opposite bank was a flat spot like a landing, from which the stair-like path started up the mesa. We women paused on the flat to draw our breath for the climb, but the children did not halt. They started running up the trail.

The little canyon here was very narrow; not quite so narrow that we could span it with out-stretched arms, but almost so. The path went up and out of sight along it, some-times rising in steep steps, sometimes flattening out like a corridor for a short distance. Trees grew along the track, junipers and stunted pines, and between them were the dwarf high-altitude cacti. The sharp thorns of the low-growing plants threatened our hands and shoes. The mesa was inhospitable. It did not refuse to receive visitors, but it managed to make their approach to intimacy difficult.

One of the little boys popped an elfish face around a bend

in the path ahead of us. "The teacher says they carried the water up this way," he proclaimed, and vanished again.

"They mus' carry the jugs on their heads if they people," Concepción observed. "We carry it from the river to the pueblo that way when we girls, my sister and I. Indians don' change much. They don' change their ways—'less they has to."

The valley floor where we started our climb was six thousand feet above sea level, and we had continued steadily upward. The children and the old woman, who had always lived at high altitudes, breathed evenly and calmly, but we lowlanders caught our breaths sharply, and found that the air came only into the upper parts of our lungs. From time to time we had to stop to rest. Concepción sat with us under the shade of a branching pine.

"This where we use' to fin' the beads," she said at one halt. "My sister was sure good at finding them. She had sharp eyes when we girls, and she always had good luck. I never could fin' the beads, but the li'l stone shells I could fin'."

"What kind of beads were they?"

"Like the shell beads the Indians make at Santo Domingo Pueblo, down the river. Li'l tubes of shell, like drums with holes bored through them. I think the li'l people of the earth drilled their beads differen' from those living Indians. I always see their holes go straight through, not taper in the middle like the ones the Santo Domingos drill now'-days."

"Like this one?" Martha asked her. She extended her hand, with a small white tube flat on its palm.

"Like that," Concepción assured her.

"Let me see it," I requested, reaching for the bead.

It was not a bead. Flat on the palm of my own hand lay a segment of crinoid stem; fossilized fragment of an under-

247

sea flower. It had lain here on the side of the mesa for un-
countable centuries.

"That was once a plant that grew on the bottom of the
ocean," I said, staring at it. "All this mesa must have been
the floor of the sea at one time."

Concepción was digging in the earth with a twig as I
spoke, and now she stretched out her own hand towards me.
"And this?" she asked.

I took the tiny shell, stone now, but still a shell in form,
and marveled over it. "That too," I said. "That once came
from the ocean. It lived there at the same time that the
flower grew."

Concepción shook her head. "Like magic. The worl'
change like magic," she said in a hushed voice. "How long
time ago was this ocean?"

"Nobody knows," I answered. "They guess but they don't
know for sure. Millions of years ago, probably. Before
human beings were even made."

"Millions of years ago," Concepción repeated. Her
wrinkled brown face cracked open with a smile. "No people
living here then, jus' the ocean and its li'l animals. Lots
things had to happen before the people came."

"People hadn't come to be then," I reiterated slowly. The
tiny shell in my palm became truly a magic thing at that
moment; a talisman that took us back beyond human kind
into a day of the ocean water's limitless cleanness.

"Only the li'l people of the earth," Concepción reminded
me. "They the only ones was here in those times then."

We did not argue with her. How should we question what
she so surely knew? Earth spirits, magic, power—those
things must in some way have been. Force of some sort had
been needed to raise the mesa from the ocean floor and to
banish the waters from the face of the land. The Indian

woman had the same right to name that force that we had. The force lost none of its strength by being named.

We left the tide level behind us as we climbed again. The trees were sparser now, not set so closely together nor growing quite so large. The spaces between the trees were filled with coarse bunch grass; there were fewer cacti. The mesa had done what it could to repel us, and we had not surrendered. We had continued along our course. Now, without welcoming, the mesa tolerated us. It was beginning to understand, as I was.

"We never came this high when we were young," Concepción said presently. She had paused just ahead of us, and when we reached the point where she stood, we saw why she had stopped. We were on a cliff overlooking the ocean— a gray-brown-green rolling floor, desert now, but no more barren than it must first have been. Desert of water, desert of land, they had the same smooth, even flow, the same rolling, waxen curve that followed the curve of space, the same finite infinity as they touched horizons.

"It hasn't changed much after all," Martha almost whispered, and Concepción caught at the half-spoken thought, and asked,

"Is the ocean really like this?" She had no need to tell us that she, whose life had been only with mountains, had never seen an ocean.

"Very much like this," Martha said. "It has a different color—a lot of different colors. That's all."

"There aren't colored trees to make streaks across an ocean," I reminded her, and Martha shrugged.

"You can find differences if you look for them," she conceded. "The wonderful thing is that they are so much alike."

"The worl' changes more than people do," said Concepción. Then she went on, "We near the top, I think," and without more words went on along the upward path ahead. Again we climbed and climbed, until again Concepción stopped. "I los' the path," she said. "There that big rock ahead of us, but I don' see nothin' else."

"Here are the children's footprints," I noticed, stooping down. The small marks of sturdy shoes were clear on the bare earth, and beside them, equally clear, were tiny cloven prints. "Deer still come this way, and the boys have followed the deer trail," I added. "This is the way they went. Stoop under the rock, here, where it shelves. Yes, here's a kind of path. We can follow it."

Behind me I heard Concepción laugh. "It take sharp eyes to follow trail like that," she observed. "If people live up here, they be safe. Enemy couldn' get pas' that gate if the people want to stop them. They say the Indians buil' Acoma Pueblo plan it that way too, so it be safe."

We rounded the rock, and then we found we were on top of the mesa. Its rim curved upward, saucer-like, behind us, when we took a few tentative forward steps, and we stood in a slight hollow. We were without the view across the valley floor, and we saw nothing before us but the same junipers and pine trees that had surrounded us as we climbed. None of us was quite prepared for so dull an outlook, and we were all disappointed. Concepción stopped a moment, then stepped forward and took the lead again.

"There's no path here," she said after a moment, "and I can't see the children's footprints. You look, and see if you fin' out where they gone."

We both searched; we went back to the place where we had come out on the top of the mesa and tried to trail the boys from there. Our own footprints had obliterated theirs. We rejoined Concepción.

"We'd better call to them," Martha said, and so we all called and whistled, but no answers came.

"Li'l gophers!" Concepción exclaimed. "They come out when it time to eat lunch. I guess they be playing games somewhere till then. Right now seems like they gone underground, like the ole people."

"Let's look around and see what we can find, now we're here," Martha suggested. "The mesa top can't be very big. We can at least see if there ever were an old pueblo here."

"I'm going to mark the path," I said. "You're probably right, and the mesa top isn't very big, but I don't think it would be any fun to go around and around the edge looking for a path under a rock that looked like every other rock, especially after it begins to get dark."

I tied the red bandana I had been wearing for a neckerchief to a juniper tree at the head of the trail, and Concepción nodded.

"If the boys come back and see that, they know where we are," she said approvingly.

"Which way do you think we ought to go?" Martha asked.

"East," Concepción promptly informed her. "Good spirits come from east, so people always live in that direction. That the way we ought to go."

The top of the mesa was not round, as I had expected it to be. Instead, it ran in a long oval from west to east. We had come up about the middle of the north side, and from where we stood it would have been as easy to go in one direction as another. We followed Concepción's guidance, and went forward over the slightly roughed, but almost level, ground.

"People have been here," Martha remarked, leaning forward. She lifted something from the earth, and a moment

251

later held out to us a small piece of black-and-white painted pottery. Concepción looked at it, and shook her head.

"That not from our pueblo," she said. "Some strange Indians mus' been here. We never made that kind of pottery."

"Whoever made it brought it here a long time ago," I observed. "That kind of pottery hasn't been made for hundreds of years."

"It fresh," Concepción argued. "Look. The colors so clear. That was a good pot when it was made. It can't be very ole."

"It must be old," I insisted. "Pottery colors don't change with time. It was made a long, long time ago."

"Everything is so ole," Concepción murmured. "I am an ole woman and you young. I don' remember seeing pottery like that ever before. You tell me the pottery hundreds years ole and the shell beads millions years ole. When you as ole as I am years will mean more to you. Changes will mean more, too."

She led the way in silence for almost a mile, threading her way through the scattered small trees as surely as if she were crossing the plaza of her own pueblo. Here and there and now and then we picked up other bits of pottery, all painted like the first one Martha found.

"There are birds!" Martha exclaimed suddenly, stopping in her tracks. "Birds up here, in October! I can hear them! Where are they?"

I stopped, too, and listened. Then I laughed. "It's the children. They must be up ahead there," I said. "You can hear them laughing."

"Yes," agreed Concepción. "It my li'l boys." She, too, listened. "They foun' something," she added, and lifted her voice in a clear call. An answering call came back. "We foun' them," she remarked in a relieved tone. "They haven't gone underground. Everything else has, the li'l people of the earth and the ole-time Indians, but my li'l boys still on top the mesa."

We followed the call, sounding nearer to us now, and reached an opening in the trees. There before us we saw the children. They were sitting on a low mound, digging in its top with sticks. Other low mounds extended on either hand about a square open space before us, and in the center of the plaza—for it could be nothing else—a single, higher mound stood all alone.

"It's the ole pueblo, Gran'ma," one of the children said. "Look," he went on, "we found something." He showed us more pieces of broken painted pottery, and small fragments of chipped stone. One of the scraps gleamed with the glassy sheen of fractured obsidian.

"These were the houses," another child said. "Look, they went all around the plaza like a wall. Why did they build one house all by itself in the middle, do you think?"

"They went around the plaza like a wall," Concepción repeated. "The same way the houses use to go all 'roun' the plaza in our pueblo. That mus' have been the *kiva* in the middle, where they worshiped. They were people who live' here then. One time I guess the houses stood above the earth. Now they gone underground."

"The earth has come up and covered them," Martha said wonderingly.

"It was all so long ago, the earth has buried them."

"It was all so long ago," Concepción reiterated. "And still they people like us. They Indians like us. They brought their water up from the river, the way we use to do, and they buil' their house 'roun' the plaza in the Indian way, with the *kiva* in the middle where it ought to be. All so long ago, and still they people like us. Indians don' leave their houses 'less they mus'. What happen to them?"

253

"Maybe they moved away," I offered. "Maybe there was a drought summer and the river went dry, and they had to leave. Or maybe the insects came and crops were spoiled, so they had to go where things would grow. Maybe, even, a sickness came and people began to die, so those who were left moved to a safer place."

Concepción nodded gravely. "Maybe lots of things," she said. "Maybe that ole ocean came up to swallow them and they swam away. Maybe they went underground same as those stone shells did. Maybe the time came to end living here and to go on. Some day maybe they come back. Indians know how. They can do them things and keep their beliefs safe. When the people ready, maybe they come back, and their crops grow from this earth, and this town live again. Indian towns don' die. They change like this worl', but they don' die."

This, then, was the secret of the mesa. It held, along its sides and on its top, a record of a few of the many changes that had assailed the world and its peoples since their earliest beginnings. No single small mesa could preserve every change, but what it could hold, this one had kept. Now, I thought, the mesa and I understood each other; now tolerance and confidence were established between us. Mentally, I shook hands with the little mesa every step of the way down its side to lunch beside the river that flowed past its base.

CHAPTER 19

FATES TEMPTED

THE acid test of an ethnologist's relations with a tribe he has studied is whether or not he can go back. It has always been a matter of intense pride to me that I could return at will to the group of Indians whom I first studied, and could come and go among them, at once an honored guest and a member of the family. This was true even after I had published two books on the tribe, a time when, if ever, I should have been cast with scoffing into outer darkness.

Off and on, the processes of studying and writing about the one tribe occupied a period of ten years, and my comings and goings since then have extended over most of another ten. I have seen the people who were old when I first came to visit them die, the mature age, and the youngsters grow up. I have worked and studied with many other tribes, and have returned to compare their ways with those I knew first and still know best.

All sorts of changes have occurred in these nearly twenty

years, and I have not yet, and presumably never will, come to the end of surprises in connection with this particular Plains Indian tribe. Nor do I particularly want to. It would be an exceedingly dull life if one realized that one had come to the end of the information the world offers about any single topic.

So when my friend Elizabeth wrote to me, a couple of summers ago, and invited me down to spend the week of the Indian Fair with her and her family, I accepted happily. I had been to lots of Indian Fairs in previous years, and had always enjoyed them. Sometimes I camped on the fair grounds with Elizabeth's family, sometimes I stayed at a tourist court. This year I found quarters at the Government Indian school. I knew that Elizabeth could and would make room for me, but it might involve setting up an extra tent and all the trouble that could entail. It was simpler for me to have headquarters in a dormitory room, and return to it at night.

I drove down to Agency Town the morning before the fair opened. Just outside the town the highway passed the fair grounds—a five-acre expanse of level prairie, with the curve of a concrete grandstand and the opposed curves of half a dozen tipis looming above its flatness. I continued past the camp and on through the town, to establish myself in my room at school.

As I drove into the camp an hour later, I was aware of something unusual in its atmosphere. There was more than the usual bustle and stir of preparation for the parade and pageant. Women moved back and forth between their tents and brush arbors, busy cooking on the gasoline stoves they had set out in the open. Some women carried pressure-cookers with them from the shelters to the fires; others turned slabs of beef ribs, roasting aboriginally over hickory

coals, with forked sticks. Children and dogs played and
tumbled, rolling underfoot and out again as Indian children
and dogs have done for approximately twenty thousand
years. The old men sat on army cots in the shade, solemnly
inhaling corn-shuck cigarettes, solemnly spitting into holes
in the ground. Dance costumes, hung on clothes lines
strung between tents and arbors, twisted in a blaze of color
of aniline-dyed chicken feathers, and spun in the wind with
a sharpening tinkle of bells and mirrors. Outwardly this camp
was as it had always been.

But an intangible current stirred into tenseness beneath
the atmosphere of relaxation. How I knew that this was not
the time of gaiety and nonsense that it usually was, I could
not have told. Anxiety was there somewhere, chilling the
blaze of the August afternoon, entering my nostrils and
prickling them with the dust that drifted everywhere.

I threaded the car through the lanes left between the
lines of shelters until I reached Elizabeth's camp, on the
southwest periphery of the huddle. Her father and mother
had camped in that same spot when she was a child; Grandmother had pitched her tipi in the same relative position in
the old camp circle, I had been told. By right of inheritance
and maintenance this place was Elizabeth's, away from the
worst of the dust and the noise and the crowd, sheltered
from the earliest sunlight by other tents and arbors.

Elizabeth and I exchanged the ritual embrace of sisters
meeting after parting, laying our cheeks against each others'
for an instant. I looked around me, and saw that we were
alone in the camp. The rest of the family was away for the
moment, and I was glad it was so. Since Elizabeth had left
the government service to concentrate on bringing up her
own children, we seldom had a chance to talk to one another
alone during my brief visits to the Kiowa country.

257

So now we dropped down on a bench under the shelter of the arbor, and exchanged news of the usual kind. The children and Elizabeth's husband were well, she was substitute teacher in the government community school near her home; her stepmother had had a cold earlier in the summer but was better by now; a new chain store had opened in Agency Town and the prices of groceries were lower than they had been for years. I told of my father's long illness and recent death; of my mother's health; the progress of nieces and nephews in school; my plans to lecture at an eastern museum that fall.

Around us the light slanted more level and more golden as we spoke. The dust drifted along the air currents, and hickory smoke moved with it like incense from a censor in a slowly swinging hand. We came to the end of the immediate news and paused, to listen for a moment to voices more distant than our own.

"What is it, Elizabeth?" I asked. "What's gone wrong?"

Elizabeth did not answer me directly. "Sometimes I think education is an awful mistake for Indians," she said. The obliqueness of the remark indicated a reversion of old tribal patterns of speech, and that, in turn, meant that something was seriously wrong.

I banally quoted Pope, to the effect that a little learning is a dangerous thing, and Elizabeth nodded.

"I know," she said. "Freshman English." Her hand began to pat the surface of the bench beside her—the gesture of a palm stroking a drum head. I could remember her grandmother's hand in the same gesture, the first summer I knew Elizabeth. I waited.

"A *little* learning isn't always dangerous," she said at last. "A lot of learning about some one thing—and nothing else —can be worse. The kind that shuts out everything else.

When you learn so much about new facts that you forget what you should know about old beliefs—then learning can be terribly dangerous."

"Who has forgotten?" I inquired, gazing out across the camp. Not for anything would I have offended against the old-fashioned tribal etiquette by looking straight at Elizabeth at a moment like this.

"Bradford Wright," she answered, her eyes still following her patting hand.

"Bradford Wright." The name was vaguely familiar, and I repeated it, trying to place it. "Bradford Wright. Oh, yes. The boy at the university. Taking his degree in mathematics."

"That's the one," Elizabeth agreed. "Only, he switched his major. Advanced mathematics were too much for an Indian, I guess. He's taking his master's degree in education. He wants to teach in a Government school."

"Fine!" I said heartily. "He'll do a lot better for himself and much more for other people by teaching than he could if he stuck in a physics laboratory."

Elizabeth turned on me with a long, and very direct, look. "Are you sure?" she demanded.

"What do you mean?"

"Have you ever seen my tribe do the Sun Dance?"

I laughed. "I have not, and neither have you. The last Sun Dance was given in 1892, according to Dr. Mooney, and neither of us can claim to have been there."

"What do we know about the Sun Dance?"

I thought back along the string of years, to the summer when Elizabeth and I first worked together. "Your old uncle told us more about it than anyone else did," I hazarded. "None of the old people—the *real* old people—especially wanted to talk about it. But Uncle said that it was the most

259

important dance the tribe had ever had, and that it was given so the buffalo would thrive and there would be plenty of meat for everyone during the coming year. He said then that the Sun Dance god was still alive and was still being cared for by the man who had inherited the right to watch over it.

"The dance had to end when it did—in 1892, the year the Indians went to dance at the first Chicago World's Fair—because the one man who had the most important place in the ceremony had died and had left no heirs. But all the other people who had the right to take part in the ceremony were still alive then, including the man who guarded the Sun Dance god, and as far as I know their descendants were alive when Uncle talked to us about it. I suppose there are still descendants of descendants around."

"What did Uncle tell us about dancing and singing the Sun Dance songs?"

Again I had to dredge my memory. "He used to sing Sun Dance songs to us sometimes, and so did Grandmother. Oh, I remember now. You can sing the songs in the summertime, when the dance used to be held. Men and women can sing them. Lots of people probably still do. But you can't dance to them. And you can't put up a circular arbor —ever—because that is a Sun Dance arbor, and can only be put up with the right ceremonies."

"What happens if you put up a round arbor or dance Sun Dance steps without the ceremonies?"

"In the old days the Sun Dance was a healing rite, as well as one to bring food. If it were done properly, you made a vow that if someone in your family, very near to you, recovered from a sickness or returned from a war raid you would give the dance. And if the vow were fulfilled, you and your friends danced and fasted from food and water

260

during four days and nights. Then you and your family and the whole tribe could look forward to a year of health and happiness and prosperity. But if anything went wrong—if there were any tiny slip in the dancing or if your vow were not sincere—if anyone ate or drank and continued to dance —there would be a curse on everybody. Some person you loved would die, and the whole tribe would have a year of misfortune."

"Do you believe all that?" Elizabeth fired at me.

"Do you?"

Elizabeth's hand was stilled, her head down-bent. "I'm a Christian," she said. "I believe in all the articles of the Christian faith, as you say. But *still* I wouldn't like to offend the old gods. They were here first. People walked this earth believing in them for centuries. Belief is power. Some of it could be left behind. I don't believe in the old gods as living gods, no. But I wouldn't like to insult them. I wouldn't be afraid my children would die, or anything like that—nor my parents, if they were living—but I wouldn't want to break the old rules."

That was a comprehensive answer. I looked across the camp, stirring always with summer wind and the movement of people, and considered.

"Why did Bradford decide to put on the Sun Dance, Elizabeth?"

"Well," said Elizabeth thoughtfully, "the fair board asked him to take charge of the program from his community, for the night dancing. You know, they ask a different person each year, and everyone who has the job tries to put on a different dance. And they've done the old reliable scalp dance, and war dances, and rabbit dances, and sometimes they've given them different names that haven't fooled anybody, for years. Everybody who comes to the fair loves them, because they're gay and colorful, with lots of good loud banging on the drums and hopping up and down and bright costumes flapping around. But Bradford decided that this year he'd *really* do something different, and he's going to put on the Sun Dance."

"Where did he get a description of it? There can't be anybody alive now who's seen it."

"Out of your book."

"Oh." This was more responsibility than I was prepared to accept immediately.

"He said," Elizabeth relentlessly continued, "that if the dance—every bit of it, including the sacred ceremonies—had been described to a white woman so clearly that she could write it down, then it must be dead, and perfectly safe for anyone to do."

"But Elizabeth! We *never* heard anything about the secret ceremonies. Nobody ever told us about them. They never told us the Sun Dance legend. Women don't know those things, and we didn't claim to."

Elizabeth nodded. "I know it. I went and got out the book and looked that chapter up, to make sure. You were perfectly honest about it; you told the truth. You described just exactly what anyone walking around in the camp during the four days of the Sun Dance could have seen. Only, you described it so clearly, anyone who read the book would think you knew a lot you hadn't put down. And that's what Bradford thought."

"Oh, Lord!"

"I know," said Elizabeth again, sympathetically. She got up from the bench. "Let's go ahead now and get dinner. Jim and the children will be back pretty soon. I told them to stay away until I had a chance to talk to you." She handed

262

me a pan of potatoes and a paring knife. "Here. You get started on these while I get the other things ready."

I sat jabbing at the potatoes with the knife, trying to convince myself that I had no responsibility for the impending Sun Dance; trying to perceive and name that share of the responsibility that could be mine.

"Hasn't anybody tried to stop him, Elizabeth? What about his father?"

"His father's all for it. You know he's been away a lot. He went east to Carlisle to school when he was a boy, and the Quakers taught him that those old beliefs were all superstitions. Then he worked for the railroad and traveled all over the country on his job, and he's as much out of touch with the rest of us as Bradford is. The two of them might just as well be a couple of white men. So Bradford's father thinks the Sun Dance is the same as any other dance, and he's encouraging his son to go ahead and destroy one more thing that belongs to the old days. He isn't a bit afraid of what could happen to him. Who's that coming?"

In all the movement of the camp she had singled out the one concerted movement. A group of women—four of them —were coming towards us. All were elderly. One had almost white hair, and another walked with a cane. All four were dressed in clean cotton prints, made in the Mother Hubbard style the missionaries had introduced sixty years or so before, and all had shawls thrown over their shoulders.

"Old Lady Red Bird, Old Lady Blue Jay, Straight-Walking Woman, and Mrs. John Smith," Elizabeth said under her breath. "Now, what do *they* want?"

The old women continued deliberately towards us, and stood before the arbor, looking anywhere but at us. Etiquette prescribed the boundaries of the family living quarters. Our

263

visitors stood rigidly beyond them, within earshot of greeting, but out of hearing of casual conversation. One of them called aloud in her own language.

"Come in," Elizabeth answered in the same tongue. She gestured them forward into the arbor, seated them on its west side in the place reserved for honored guests, and pulled the coffee pot onto a lighted burner of the camp stove. There was a pause, while she got out white enamel cups and opened a can of milk. Sugar she brought in a paper bag, and with it wood-fibre spoons. When we were all supplied with coffee, she passed around a package of cookies. There was no word spoken until the cups had been emptied. Then Straight-Walking Woman, evidently spokeswoman by prearrangement, began.

"She says," reported Elizabeth, falling into our long-established pattern, "that there is something they want to speak to you about."

"I am listening," I replied formally.

"They say that they are old women and you are a young one. In the old days, people thought that the old people knew best. Now times have changed, and the young know more than the old."

I recognized the gambit. It had opened many conversations before; conversations that led to requests to have children sent to school; to have children sent home from school; to have sons discharged from the army; to loans of petty cash. I returned my standard answer:

"Each of us can learn from others. That is why we are all in the world together."

"They say that when they were young women growing up, the Sun Dance had gone underground like the buffalo. Nobody in their generation has seen it, and they were all too

264

busy staying alive to listen to the old men talk about it when the old men were still here."

"I see."

"So you know more about their old days and their old ways than they do, because you had time to listen to the old men's words. And you know more about the modern days because you live in them and have grown up in the modern world. They grew up between two worlds, and they are not sure, till today, in which world they live."

"That is a tragedy. It happens to people sometimes and it is always tragic."

"They want you to put together your knowledge of the two worlds you know and they do not, and tell them what ought to be done about this Sun Dance."

I hesitated. "Tell them," I said at last, "that in the world where the Sun Dance had power, it was a dance for men. It was men's business. Women had no part in it, except to look on and encourage the dancers."

"But, they want to know, what would happen if the men didn't care and the women did? Would the women have the right to take part then?"

"I think not."

"What could the women do to stop it?"

"They could talk to the men in their own families, and try to persuade them not to take part."

There was a murmur among the old women, a quick exchange of nods and half-breathed words.

"They have done that. Some of the men dropped out, but eight or sixteen of the boys still say they are going to dance."

"What do you want me to do?"

"Ask the agency superintendent to stop the dance."

"I know what he will say. He cannot. The Constitution of this country says that all men have the right to worship in their own ways. The Sun Dance is a religious dance, even after all these years underground. If the superintendent tries to stop it, he will be breaking the law."

"Can he talk to the young men and *ask* them not to dance?" Elizabeth inquired after another conference among the women.

"He can do that."

"Can you ask him to do it?"

Again I deliberated. I scarcely knew this particular superintendent, he was new since my day. I did know that he was tremendously busy. How much time he would accord a stranger for the discussion of such a matter, I did not know. I offered a counter-suggestion.

"Suppose I talk to the school superintendent, and ask him to talk to the agency superintendent?"

Elizabeth relayed the question. The women beamed. They almost applauded as their spokeswoman replied.

"They say that is why they came to you. They knew that you would know the right thing to do. In the old days a question like that had to be asked four times, through two messengers. That is right. You go ahead."

I nodded. This was my responsibility, laid squarely in my lap, and not to be evaded. Our visitors rose, folded their shawls around them, and came one at a time to stand before me. They placed against my palm their own hard little palms, and walked from the arbor, still a cohesive group, but straighter and easier in motion than when they had approached us.

Jim and the children returned, and after our greetings we ate our supper almost silently. Dusk folded warm arms about us all. The sparks of the camp stoves went out, and here and there through the darkness bonfires flared. Groups of boys walked past us to rehearse for the dances the next evening, the sleighbells on their knees and ankles jingling softly in time to the faint, persistent wheezing of the merry-go-round on the fair grounds. Girls in chattering clusters, the fringes of their grandmothers' white buckskin dresses whispering softly over the dry grass, passed by us and were lost in the darkness. The children went to watch the rehearsal, and we sat with watchfulness and our own friendly silence holding us as they can only bind those who have worked hard together.

At last Elizabeth yawned a little, and rose. "You go on back to the school and go to bed," she instructed me. "Tomorrow's a big day. See if you can find those two men and talk to them before the parade starts. We'll save a place for you on the courthouse lawn, in the shade, and Jim will park the car somewhere where you can try to take pictures." She giggled. "I hope they're better than usual. All blurs. I never saw such messes."

The parade was scheduled to start at noon, which should have given me plenty of time to talk to the school superintendent, at least. But the school was entering a float that year, most of the teachers had gone home for their vacations, and the superintendent was trying to do several jobs at once. I pursued him around the school grounds, catching brief glimpses of him between the Vocational Agriculture Building and the pig pens, another flash of his reddening balding head as he organized the band for the parade, and a final tantalizing vision of him perched on the front of a hay rack that had been decked with corn stalks and bundles of wheat. He was trying to seat the school queen, whose Girl Scout uniform was already wilting in the heat, on her throne of alfalfa hay bales.

267

Finally I gave up and went back into town, to look for the agency superintendent. I was willing to defy tradition in the hope that I might fulfill my mission before parade time. But the superintendent had already left his office, and as I talked to his secretary she was closing her desk. The office would be shut for the rest of the day.

Dispiritedly, I reported to Elizabeth on the courthouse lawn. Her hand touched my shoulder, briefly and lightly as a bird's wing might brush it. "Don't worry," she consoled me. "Maybe you'll have a chance to speak to one of them this afternoon. The boys aren't going to dance until tonight. Sun Dancing in the dark! Go on and get on top of the car with Jim, so you can watch."

I scrambled over the hood and balanced myself precariously on the roof of the car. Jim, Elizabeth's husband, turned when he heard me, and held out a hand to help me slide along to a place beside him, where we sat with our feet dangling over the turtleback and looked along the street. The sun poured on us like syrup from a jug, and no straw hat was sufficient to turn it. Metal below us and the street beneath reflected the blaze and its glare fiercely against our eyeballs.

"Sure has been an awful summer," Jim remarked while we waited. "Drought from one end to the other. I don't believe it'll ever rain."

"So they're giving a Sun Dance!" I exclaimed.

"Well," Jim remarked, "they do say that in the old days, when something went wrong with the dance, it would rain a lot."

"I thought the curse was that somebody died."

"That, too. But there was likely to be a flood."

I looked above and about me. The sky was a hard blue

crockery bowl, capping our heads. "I don't think we'd better count on *that*," I observed.

There was a silence along the street, as I realized when we stopped speaking, and a silence on that street at that time was a strange thing to hear. All about the car people stood quietly, patiently waiting. There were no children running into the street, to be fetched back by mothers or older sisters. The few old people I could see were huddled in the shade of the trees on the courthouse lawn, not fringing the outer line of spectators.

It was an orderly crowd, almost overwhelmingly well behaved, but it was not a festive crowd. Rather it seemed a crowd of people jammed together to shelter in one another's presence from an anticipated blow—one that might fall at any time, but that was bound to fall.

The air was as still as the packed crowd. Dust lay in windrows, where it had dropped at twilight the evening before, along the gutters. Gum wrappers and peanut shells lay where hands had released them. Scarves knotted around necks hung rigidly in their places, as still as the flag that drooped cocoon-like along the mast before the courthouse. In all the plains there seemed to breathe no wind, and that in the plains in August was foreboding's self.

There was a thud of drums from the end of the street, a bandmaster's shrill whistle, and then we heard the put-thud of a policeman's motorcycle moving at a foot pace along the line of march. The rider did not have to wave the people back. They stayed in place along the curb, giving him plenty of room in which to pass.

Now the parade was upon us. There was a color guard from the army post, and behind them came a general, riding in a jeep. Behind the general were the four last remaining

Indian scouts, also jammed together in a jeep, their worn blue Spanish-American War uniforms showing clean and brave against the olive drab. Another flag, followed by the post fife and drum corps. Visiting Pueblo Indians, in a shiny Cadillac lent, so a sign informed us, by an automobile agency in Albuquerque.

Then a whirl of feathered dancers, unidentifiable as to tribe, followed by a group of men who sang, and beat on a great drum, as they marched. An official government car from the agency, carrying the superintendent and the head of the school. I sighed as they went by me, so near, and yet so incredibly far. So the parade passed with dancers, drummers, bands, and cars, and with no response from the waiting crowd.

Men rode past us on horses, the men in war bonnets and the paints their grandfathers had won the right to wear, the horses with their manes and tails braided with bright ribbons and feathers. And then after the riders came another huddle of dancers. Sixteen of them there were, all young men, all painted yellow from foreheads to breech clouts and on down their legs. They all wore crowns of willow, and in their hands they carried willow boughs with the wilted leaves dangling limply along the stems. Between their lips these dancers held slim, ivory-white bone whistles, on which they tooted lackadaisically if shrilly.

"Sun Dancers!" Jim exclaimed, and was silent again.

The Sun Dancers formed the last contingent of marchers. Jim and I slid down over the turtleback of the car, and joined Elizabeth and the children in the shade of the trees. The same shade lay flat on the grass around us while we ate our lunch, its only movement that imposed on it by the movement of the earth.

"Let's go on out to the fair grounds and watch the horse races," Jim said finally.

"I'm going to try—" I said. "I'll join you later. Save a place for me if you can."

"Here's your pass," said Jim, handing me a slip of paper. He was a member of the fair board that year, as he was every year.

I located the Chamber of Commerce banquet in the basement of the Methodist Church, and hung about, waiting for the Government officials to emerge. When they came out, surrounded by a perceptible aura of fried chicken and hot biscuits, they were also surrounded by a throng, and were accompanying the general. Speech with any one of them was out of the question. I trailed along behind the official entourage to the fair grounds, where I watched the big men enter their box. Later, because I was there anyway, I watched the horse races.

Even the horses seemed oppressed by the heat and stillness. They ran, but they ran, if that is possible for quarter horses, slowly. The crowd did not cheer, and few spectators placed bets. Only the owners of horses backed their stock, because it was expected of them.

I made another attempt, at the end of the afternoon program, to reach the superintendents. This time the band intervened, playing the general out of the bandstand with "The Star-Spangled Banner." I looked around me. The Committee of Four had come up out of the boards of the seats, apparently, and were standing behind me, looking at me questioningly. I shook my head and they shook theirs, sadly.

As I walked back across the fair grounds to the camp, mechanically stepping in time to the merry-go-round music,

271

it seemed to me that a space separated me from the rest of the crowd. I walked alone until I reached the shelter of Elizabeth's arbor, and the kindness of her smile. Fortified by the scalding coffee that she poured for me, I took my car and drove into town to try to telephone those two elusive men. They had taken the general to a barbecue, given by the Kiwanis Club. They could not be reached.

Silence smothered the camp. Four thousand people could not be that quiet—but they were. Only the merry-go-round, endlessly, restlessly, grinding "Over the Waves," could be heard. The Indians sat in bunches, and the low sun flared on them, turning everything and everybody in sight crimson. Far on the eastern horizon night was coming up in a sheet of blue blackness, looking at that great distance like the blackness of thunder clouds. The stillness all around us was that which pervades a country church before a funeral.

We ate store bread and cold boiled ham folded into sand-wiches, and drank more coffee. I bought a watermelon from a stand at the entrance to the camp and we hacked it open and ate it cooled by its own evaporation. The children were as quiet as the grownups. There was no visiting from tent to tent, as there normally was. We gathered the scraps of the meal together and buried them. We went, always silently, to the grandstand to find our places for the evening's per-formance.

The program started on time, an unusual phenomenon in itself. The darkness rose in the east and swallowed the first stars, eating them up as voraciously as it did the last color in the west behind us. The floodlights glared down on the racetrack, which had been cleared and scraped clean for the dancing, and on the circular enclosure at its far side, where the clutch of yellow-stained dancers sat huddled on rough board benches.

272

The Pueblo visitors danced first, dipping and sweeping in the almost static, conventionalized curves of their eagle dance. Our own young men flooded out, whooping and yelling, in a war dance. The women formed a moving wall behind them, opened their ranks to admit the men and form couples, and then they all circled in a flirtation dance. The evening was following a pattern set for us long before, familiar, and the more beautiful to us because of its familiarity.

Men brought in arm loads of wood and built a fire, and the Apaches came leaping out in their great crown-like head-dresses for the fire dance, springing high over the flames, vivid, diabolic figures, although their movements were prayers for our health and well being. The evening was well along now. Indeed, the planned entertainment was almost over.

The Apaches whirled away. The fire had died to coals, and the floodlights came on again, drenching the arbor and the figures in it. We could see that all the dancers were standing now. The first toots of the bone whistles pierced our ears as a freezing blast of wind out of the north pierced our summer clothing. Lightening blazed vertically before us in the east, from zenith to horizon, and all the lights on the fair grounds were quenched. Thunder crashed around us, drowning the first thuds of the drum at the same moment that it ended the tinkle of the merry-go-round. Rain came down in solid sheets, and blocked everyone's view of the arbor and the Sun Dancers.

Suddenly there was life in the dark grandstand. Some people laughed and others applauded. We turned our heads and spoke freely to one another for the first time in that rigid evening. We gathered the children together. Lighted by our flashlights, and presently by the headlights of cars,

273

we made our way back to camp, to shelter and to cans of hot soup.

All night, through the rain, drums tapped softly back and forth along the earth, and people sang. In the morning we saw that the round arbor had been leveled by the wind, and though the fair continued the rest of its appointed four days, the structure was not rebuilt. The Sun Dancers went home, or stayed to take part in the war and flirtation dances.

Bradford's father died a week later, of pneumonia he contracted the night of the storm. Elizabeth sent me the news in a clipping from the county weekly, folded into a letter describing the funeral.

2

970.1

MARRIOTT, ALICE L
    GREENER FIELDS

c.1

970.1

Marriott, Alice L.   c.1

Greener fields.